ASCENDANCE
BECOMING THE BEST
VERSION OF YOURSELF

Patrick Michaels

Printed in The United States of America

ISBN: 978-0-9984018-9-8

ASCENDANCE: Becoming the Best Version of Yourself /

Michaels-1st ed.

1. Philosophy. 2. Self-Help. 3. Memoir.

4. Self-Actulaization. 5. Michaels.

NFB/Amelia Press
<<<>>>
119 Dorchester Road
Buffalo, New York 14213 USA
For more information please visit
nfbpublishing.com

To Patrick Michaels 1982-2003.
Where my past events have led to the best version you
see today.

What people from all areas of the world are saying about
the novel *Ascendance*

"A book about "Phoenix Nirvana" of a man (a Chinese
saying of rebirth from extreme pain and struggle)
This a great book about determination, belief, and courage. It is a real and captivating story of a man who seems
like any ordinary person in your and my life, but he
made the great achievement of leading himself on a fulfilling life path. As his colleague and friend, I am proud
and honored to witness his solid steps toward his goals.
More importantly, from the book everyone can find the
enlightening and inspiring piece that triggers extraordi-
nary and exciting journey of their lives."

-Shuran from Beijing, China

"You won't want to put this book down! You go through a
range of emotions from fear to excitement to inspiration.
Great message of overcoming challenges that happen in
everyday life."

-Lisa from Buffalo, New York

"Inspirational book about a young man who didn't believe in failing and overcame the hardest times of his life.
This inspiring book will take you close to his heart and

show you how perseverance and faith will always lead the way. A must read."

-Martha from Cali, Colombia

"An emotional rollercoaster!" Goes to the heart and soul of the author.

–Rose from Buffalo, New York

"Intrepid and personable book. The author pours his heart out and tells his story to guide and support all who read his book. His words are heartfelt and will reach your soul."

– Samantha from Panama City, Panama

Inspiring story of hope, ambition, and love that redefines what is means to be human in a world that lacks empathy and kindness. The author writes from a place of honesty and invites his readers to be honest with themselves as they pursue their dreams.

–Tim from Buffalo, New York

"I love the novel, the message was very powerful and inspirational."

-Elaine from Buffalo, New York

"I want my life, my work, my family, I want it to mean something. If you're not making someone else's life better, then you're wasting your time. Your life will become better by making other lives better."

-Will Smith

Thank you

I want to first and foremost thank you for taking the journey with me. I hope you gain some perspective reading through my life, and took some of the valuable, but extremely difficult, lessons I had to learn along the way.

I want to thank my wife, my parents and my family, and my close friends who helped motivate me to tell my story. I want to thank Rhonda Byrne, Jack Canfield and Anthony Robbins, whom I have never met but would be honored to sit down and speak with one day. They gave me the courage to stop hiding from myself and burying my past in some dark place in my mind, and instead to be completely accountable and responsible for my past and future, along with taking a long hard look and being brutally honest with the person I saw in the mirror. With their words, I was able to open up for the greater good with a focus on helping others around the world, who have gone through what I experienced to varying degrees, and help motivate them to be better versions of themselves.

My goal in the following pages is to help and

inspire others who have hit their "ultimate rock bottom," and give them hope to carry onward and upward. My goal is to inspire people who have given up on themselves and give them something to believe in, something they can gravitate to, and use my words and my story, to pull themselves out from the depths of their personal hell in which they currently find themselves. My goal is to help bring them up to be the people they should have always been. I'm not proud of my past, but I needed to accept all of it in order to build my future. This was extremely difficult to write because I admitted many things to myself for the very first time, but I sacrificed my silence to self-heal and also in hopes of reaching others who are too afraid to face their own demons.

These experiences have forever shaped me. I wouldn't be who I am today without these events, so I look at them as "necessary evils" that I had to endure in my life. I was lost and needed something to wake me up. I needed to stop feeling that I had no control over my life, and that I was simply living in someone else's shadows, but never truly experiencing this life on my own. For that I am grateful. I thank God and the Universe every morning and every evening, expressing gratitude that I am alive to tell my story. I believe there was a purpose and reason why I had been spared and been given chance after chance. It took me many years to find out what my purpose was in this world, but I believe this is what I was meant to do with my life…inspire those who didn't or don't currently, have the courage or belief to inspire themselves.

To those who read through the following pages, from the deepest parts of my heart, thank you. I hope this book finds you when you need it the most.

Thank you

Introduction

"If your dream isn't bigger than you, then there's a problem with your dream!"

- Hall of Fame Speech by NFL great Deion Sanders

The human spirit and the human soul can endure. It can fight back when it is being attacked. It can mend and strengthen after it has been weakened. It can pull you from the depths of hell and the ultimate bottom, and take you to your "dream scenario." When you feel you have nothing left to give, it can help you rise. It can help you ascend to the person you were always supposed to be- the best version of yourself. It can help you pursue your hopes and dreams and turn them into reality.

If you commit yourself completely to what you want in this life, and go after it without fear, the human spirit will carry you there. You must give up your past, all of it, go to the depths of your mind, heart, and soul, dig through the hurt, the pain, and the sadness, to pull out the courage and dedication you have always had, but have lost along the way. You are worth it, but you must believe it. You must feel you are worth it. You must feel you deserve it. If you are willing to sacrifice, truly sacrifice, you can achieve this. This life can beat you down, it can take everything without asking, it can leave you lifeless gasping for air, it can devour you whole. This can only happen, though, IF YOU LET IT. You are in control of your life, every aspect, every moment. Your thoughts and feelings, that you control, dictate everything. Your decisions and your actions directly result in the next event in your life. It has always worked this way, and it will always work this way. You create the life you want, and no one can take that away from you, unless you let them. You decide how your story unfolds and how it ends. No one else can, just you.

For the majority of my past, I let people dictate how I felt about myself, I let them dictate how far I could go and what I could achieve. I let people talk me out of truly striving for my dreams, and going after what would make me happy. By allowing this, pain and sadness was the end result. During this time, I achieved good things but negated them by the bad decisions that I made. I paid the consequences for them all. I tried to bury or run away from my fears, my worries, and my sadness. I didn't have the courage to stand up for myself, to face myself, and confront those who opposed me.

My experiences, which you will read, have changed me, shaped me, and taught me that I have complete control over what comes next. I wish I didn't endure these events, but I believe they were needed to finally awaken me. It took massive changes in my faith, my expectations, and my beliefs, to turn my life around and have it heading in the right direction. It wasn't easy, but nothing with any significant value usually is. I had buried bad memories and sad times, and wondered why I still couldn't move forward. I decided one day that I had enough. I decided I wouldn't run away anymore, but instead, I would stand and face my past demons. The burden had become too heavy to carry. I decided to only follow one voice, instead of the many that I had before, and that one voice was my own. I decided to stop the bad things from happening by taking full ownership of my past and moving forward. I have seen the ultimate bottom, the last gasp to survive, the hopelessness, the despair. I have seen the rise of my being, the hope, and the courage restored. I am not proud of some of the decisions made in my life, but I finally owned up to them. I have finally owned up to all of them. You can do the same. It can be done. You don't need to feel that you are at the effect of the things around you. You can dictate the terms. You don't have to feel like the victim anymore. You don't have to do this alone, God knows I couldn't have survived without support from my parents, close friends, and beautiful wife. If you don't have this support system, let my words serve you. Let my words be the push and support that you need.

In my experience, my healing process began with reading of best-selling book "The Secret," written by Rhonda Byme. This inspirational book caught my attention and helped me recognize and address the lack of faith I had in religion, the outside universe, and my overall psyche. I remember when I was a little boy, watching athletes like Joe Montana and Michael Jordan on television. I would sit there and wonder how they reached the pinnacle of their respective sports. Sure they were talented, but their attention to detail, relentless work ethic, and their unwavering confidence to remain calm in pressure packed situations, is what I believe set them apart from their competition. I was always fascinated watching them in action and leading their team to victory, then I would patiently wait for the post game show to hear them speak with the media about what went through their minds in certain critical points within the game. I would always hear the words, "trust," "confidence," and the phrases similar to "expecting positive outcomes." I would replay their words in my mind, but not until I read this powerful book, did I know there was a scientifically proven process behind their ways of thinking and the results they were achieving. I didn't fully understand or appreciate the relationship I possessed with the Universe. Once I became aware of the Law of Attraction, I chose to replay and intently listen to past NFL Hall of Fame Speeches of past greats to see what they all had in common. After listening to NFL greats such as Jerry Rice, Deion Sanders, and Thurman Thomas, I realized they all thought this way and understood how to use "the law" to achieve and materialize their greatness. They all had outside influences that pushed them along the way, whether it be proving someone wrong who doubted them, bringing their family out of their past financial troubles, or to reward certain people or past coaches who believed in them. They all had something driving them, a goal larger than themselves, something or someone that they refused to disappoint. What fascinated me was that most of the players came from poor upbringings, and the average person evaluating their current situation or surroundings, would completely discount them from achieving anything noteworthy with their lives. One thing they all had in common, however, was their unwavering belief to achieve greatness. Their ability to visualize a life, much greater than their current circumstances and surroundings, was amazing to me.

One speech that had always resonated with me is when I listened to the great cornerback Deion Sanders. He stood confidently at the Hall of Fame podium in Canton Ohio and stated, "The difference between me and some of you children, some of you adults, is that I expect to be great." He would later go on to say, "Expect what you desire." Once I heard these words, it stopped me immediately in my tracks. So much so, that I had to replay it again countless times. He understood and mastered the law of attraction to the fullest extent. He grew up with a mother who worked several jobs, one of which being in a hospital, where she walked up and down the halls pushing a cart to clean up the facility. Deion made it his sole mission, a promise to himself, to make sure that one day *he* would be the reason why she stopped pushing that cart. He understood that the promise he made to himself was a responsibility, one that he had to take full ownership of. His speech was moving because I finally heard it from a different perspective.

The process of self-healing continued on with reading, "Money: Master the Game" by Anthony Robbins and "The Success Principles" written by Jack Canfield, who provided me with vital information on how to save and create wealth through commonly used financial products like index funds, and made me look deep inside myself to what motivated me to want to create wealth and prosperity in my life, along with the deep rooted relationship I had with money and the means that wealth would help me achieve. My self-healing progressed exponentially further with the completion of this book.

This healing process helped me put the past away for good and allowed me to fully and truly move on. I could have let this story stay in the shadows, in some closet or shelf to never be read again, but that does no good to the millions of people that this could benefit.

The armor is off, the guard is down, I am completely exposed, and truthfully, I have never felt more at peace than in this moment. I believe this is what it took for me to start achieving and receiving. My life is smeared across these pages for the world to see. The story needs to be told.

Thank you for taking the journey with me and I hope you find value in the pages ahead. Are you ready? Let's do this together.

This is my life. This is my journey. This is my story.

Chapter 1:
Emergency Surgery

"The best lessons I ever learned in life came from the worst experiences in my life."
- Author John Assaraf

How did I get here? How did I get to this point? How is my life no longer my own, no longer in my hands, but instead entrusted into God's? How am I at the point where I have no control, no say in what happens next? How am I at the crossroads where I don't know if I'll wake up or if these are truly the final moments when I will be in this life, this earth, this reality? There are so many things left undone, left unfulfilled. This isn't the way it ends, not for me…is it?

Looking up at the ceiling of the emergency surgery room located within Sister's Hospital—ironically, the same hospital I was born in nineteen years ago—could also be my final resting place. While lying there all I see is one color: white. Eye piercing white, a color that is so bright against my blue eyes that it is difficult to see, difficult to focus. The images in my mind are coming in so quickly. The only images that seem to stick are snapshots of my childhood.

First, I remember one picture, from my parent's photo album of my first birthday. The image of me eating the large white frosted cake that said "Happy Birthday Patrick" in blue lettered icing that included a carousel theme displaying brown, black, and white horses. I had frosting all over my lips and left hand, with my arm and index finger pointed to the sky, declaring to the world the age I had just turned.

There are things that I have achieved to this point, like consistently making the honors list at Saint Francis High School, and numerous awards in hockey throughout my childhood at Hamburg, West Seneca, and in high school.

However, if my life would come to an abrupt end, it would leave so many goals left unattained. So many experiences like the accomplishments of graduating college, finding a successful career, getting married, and starting my own family. All these experiences would be left unfulfilled.

My mind quickly takes me to another flashback, to just one year prior to my current urgent situation. I was at center ice of the college ice rink in Watertown, New York, celebrating with my teammates after our Buffalo Hornets AA team went undefeated and won the New York State Hockey Championship for the 18U Boys Midget Hockey age group by a 5-4 score. Down 4-1 in the third period, our team rattled off four straight goals, capped off by Joe Mills slamming home the rebound with just over a minute left to play.

Moments later—flying over the bench, embracing teammates that had become closer than family, team-mates that had gone through four years of three mile runs in the dead of August, with temperatures in the nineties, then going indoors to lift weights and continue on-ice strength and conditioning. Going through those enduring times, all in hopes of having the ability to play in that moment, to achieve that goal in the final week of May. It would culminate this chapter of my hockey career the way it was meant to be concluded: with a New York State Championship Title!

My mind takes me onto the next step: off to Arvada, Colorado to play in the USA National Hockey Tournament and sharing the moment with line mates I played with for years—my center man Kevin Shields, the left winger Adam Radens, while I was on the right wing side. Our line was amazing; no one could do it better. I loved playing on the "black line," representing the color of our practice jerseys. We would make several no-look passes, quickly moving down the ice, resulting in beautiful highlight reel goals with unbelievable frequency. This was achieved because we knew where the others would be in all situations due to having built an undeniable level of trust in one another. These were teammates who I first learned to skate with when we were little kids, taking our first steps on the ice, whose relationship and passion for the sport only grew stronger as we progressed through the higher levels of competition.

My mind is racing. My fourth memory, that I can recall, is at my grandfather's funeral. Standing over the coffin of the man I was named after, saying I would carry him with me always, telling him how I missed him and would see him again. Hoping he was proud of the young man I had become. How I wished we had more time, but happily knowing he would watch over me.

This is what the mind does when your body is in shock, experiencing extreme pain and is deeply entrenched in the moment of life altering uncertainty: the mind goes to another place, a better time, a better moment. I can control these precious seconds; these are mine to keep. What will happen next though, I do not control, I do not own.

The past memories of better times try to help numb my pain. These memories help prepare me for what is about to happen next. This mental preparation is required when emergency surgery is needed to help a patient survive after a spleen ruptures and massive internal bleeding is occurring. All I can do is hope for the best, but acknowledge the pain and suffering I am enduring will end very soon; one way or another, there will be a conclusion. This pain, however, is nothing like what I am going to put my family through, the pain they will endure if I do not survive. It is not about my pain anymore, it's about theirs.

My mind goes back into one final flashback, replaying the events that led me onto a gurney, fighting for my life. I thought to myself, "How could this happen? How could I get to this point?"

I got into this hectic and time sensitive predicament because I didn't listen to my body two weeks prior. I was feeling very fatigued. The more I slept, the more tired I would become. I had trouble exercising due to shortness of breath. I never experienced this before, and didn't know what was wrong with me or with my body. I would be at hockey practice, going through on-ice drills, but after a few minutes, I would be bent over gasping for air. It didn't make sense. Why was this happening?

After a few days, I noticed my ribcage on the right hand side was beginning to protrude out. My stomach, or so I thought, was continuing to expand and feeling more and more sensitive to the touch. I ignored this sign and continued to practice, go to class in college, and continue on with my normal routine. I decided to play through the pain, like so many times before, and participate in that evening's game on the Fredonia campus. As the warmups ended and I stood on the blue line, awaiting the national anthem and beginning of the first period, I was already out of breath. I continued to ignore the fatigue and played through my first shift.

After thirty seconds, I was back on the bench beginning to feel okay, as I began to get into the flow of the game. When I went out for my second shift, hopping over the boards and skating towards center ice, I received the pass from my defenseman positioned on my right hand side. As I cradled the pass and began heading up ice through the neutral zone, I was stuck by an opposing player's helmet directly on my right side. I had taken thousands of body checks to my chest and abdomen area before, but this one dropped me to the ice. This wasn't the same type of contact, as the thud of his helmet meeting my abdomen had much more impact, since that area of my body was already sensitive. As I got up off the ice and tried to head into the neutral zone, my side started to throb. The opponents' net felt so far away and I didn't have the strength to go and try scoring a goal. Instead, I headed towards the bench holding my side. As I entered the bench, the training assistant immediately came to my aid and asked what was wrong. I was starting to wince in more pain as I kept holding my right side. Then for the first time, as he began to ask me follow up questions, I started to dry heave, but my reflux refused to generate vomit. That was it, my night was over. I remained on the bench for the next stoppage in play, which felt like eternity, then started to rush with the trainer's assistance towards the locker room. Once all my equipment was off, he pressed on my side and I felt the extreme pain and sensitivity as my face grimaced further. I could feel the pain shoot up my nerve endings from my side into the top of my shoulder blade. The trainer knew something was wrong and instructed my father, who was in the stands, to take me immediately to the local hospital.

When we arrived at the hospital, I was given a room to wait while a doctor was handling other patients. The nurse came in and asked me how I was feeling and what my pain threshold was at that moment from zero to ten, ten being excruciating. It hurt, it was painful, but I felt it was not excruciating, so my response was eight.

That was a mistake. I should have said ten since I needed more urgent care, but I didn't want to admit the pain was too much to endure. As a result, my father and I sat in the waiting room for over an hour without seeing a physician. My dad went out into the hall to ask for a doctor to take a look, but they were all busy handling more urgent matters. We continued to wait for another hour, until I felt the pain starting to subside, then I made another crucial mistake by leaving the hospital. My father would make the forty-five minute drive back home to Hamburg; we would go to the hospital the next morning, since I had not received any medical attention the few hours before.

As we arrived home, I slowly went up the flight of stairs towards the shower, since I had been perspiring from the game and nervousness from the events that were unfolding. I walked past the toilet, taking a few more steps heading towards the shower. Suddenly, the nauseous feeling and pain in my side returned with much more potency this time, so I quickly rushed towards the toilet, bent over, and prepared to vomit. I could feel my abdomen tense up as my body simulated the act of throwing up, but once again nothing generated.

I could hear my throat and chest groan as if to throw up again, then all of a sudden, my balance was completely thrown off and my body went straight towards the toilet head first. I had lost all feeling in my body. I felt completely fatigued and lifeless as my skull struck the porcelain. I had no strength in my body as I reached out my hand to feel my forehead where the impact had been made. Once I saw the blood on my hand, my body went immediately into shock. I lost all motor activity in my body. I could see and understand what was happening but I couldn't control my movements. My head would continue to strike the porcelain toilet, over and over again. I could hear the thud of my skull making contact as the blood started to flow from my forehead down past my eye and down my cheek, dripping onto the floor.

I knew this was happening, I could see it, but I couldn't stop it. Over and over, what must have been five or six times, until my body flew back, resulting in me lying face up towards the ceiling. I was helpless and knew something was severely wrong. I was desperate. I needed help. I tried calling out to my family, but the groans were falling upon deaf ears. As my eyes started to close for what could be the last time, my sister abruptly rushed into the room. She had heard the noise from downstairs and rushed up to help. She saw me lying there as the blood continued to gush from my head.

"Oh my God, Patrick!" she screamed. "Mom! Dad! Call an ambulance!"

All I heard after that were sporadic voices coming in and out of my consciousness. My sister, who worked as a Physician Assistant, was perfectly trained for this type of situation, as she helped me off the floor and into her room that was located around the left corner.

As she laid me on her bed and stared into my eyes, she could see the life draining from my face and body as I could hear briefly "He's grey, he's turning grey, where is that ambulance?!"

This was the last thing I could remember before re-gaining consciousness at the hospital, after being rushed into the operating room on a gurney by the emergency ambulance. My life could have ended on the upstairs bathroom of my home if it wasn't for my sister Michele. She saved my life. In those frantic moments, she gave me the opportunity and the slim chance to survive. She was my guardian angel, but would I ever have the chance to thank her?

As my mind and body continue to replay these events, I am abruptly shaken by the words "Are you ready? Do you know what is happening Patrick? We're going to try and save you...see you when you wake up." These were the last words the surgeon said to me as he looked down with a concerning face that lacked the confidence one would expect to see from a surgeon with twenty years of experience. In that final moment, before the anesthesia sets in, all I could see in my mind was my parents. I could picture their concerned faces. I could see them trying to keep it together and trying to be strong for me.

The only feeling or wish that I have was hoping I could return to them. All I needed was a second chance, an opportunity to do things differently, to set things right. I needed help, I needed to be saved, I needed a miracle.

CHAPTER 2:
ROAD TO RECOVERY?

*"Let me tell you something you already know. The world
ain't all sunshine and rainbows. It's a very mean and nasty
place. I don't care how tough you are. It will beat you to
your knees and keep you there permanently there if you let
it. You, me, or nobody, is gonna hit as hard as life, but it
ain't how hard you're hit. It's about how hard you can get
hit and keep moving forward. How much you can take and
keep moving forward. That's how winning is done. Now
if you know what you're worth, then go out and get what
you're worth, but you have to be willing to take the hits
and not point fingers saying you're not where you want to
be because of him or her or anybody. Cowards do that and
that ain't you. You're better than that!"*
—*Sylvester Stallone in Rocky Five*

I am starting to come to, my eyes are starting to
focus and regain a picture of what I believe is
reality. Am I alive? Did I make it through? I'm not quite

33

sure. The picture before me is scrambled, but as it starts to generate a clearer image, the once perfectly white view starts to have a more dominant red color to it. What is that?

My eyes continue to focus a little more. The red color is in a circular shape and becoming clearer as the anesthesia begins to wear off. Focusing further, I begin to hauntingly realize that this dark red before me is indeed blood. A mound of blood-soaked towels are on top of the counter to the far left of me.

Suddenly a sharp pain in my abdomen steals my focus away from the blood soaked towels. I am terrified to look down, as I'm not prepared and not strong enough emotionally to deal with what I may see. My eyes start to head south, inch by inch towards my abdomen. Passing the chest, getting closer to the source of the excruciating pain, then……WHAM! The nurse put her hand on my forehead, slamming the back of my head back towards the operating table.

"Doctor, the anesthesia is wearing off…Patrick… Patrick you have to stay flat, you must remain still. We're finishing up the closure process!" Then a mask was put over my mouth and I could feel the influx of air flowing into my mouth then into my lungs…silence. Back to stillness.

Was this real? Am I imagining this? Did I wake up before the operation was completed? I wasn't prepared to see the open incision that was seven inches long, going up from my belly button up to the bottom of my chest.

The next few hours of events would be relayed to me from speaking with my parents— absent from my memory, of course, since I was still under from the strong narcotic called Dilaudid that was pumped into my bloodstream.

After surgery, I was taken into a recovery room and was stabilized, then after a few more hours, I was moved into the surgical intensive care unit. It was there, for a few minutes, that a couple members of my family would come to visit to me.

When I finally came to several hours later, I was in my hospital room lying on a large recovery bed with a bouquet of flowers on the side table, and my parents and sister in full view to greet me when the anesthesia had finally worn off. I had made it; I had been saved. I was here in reality, but I had to make sure. I pointed to my mother, directing her near and close enough, so the faint whisper leaving my chapped lips could be heard.

"Am I dead?" I asked.

She replied, "God no, you are here with us, we're so happy you made it. We love you, that's all you need to know right now." A calming ease rushed over my body. I had made it through.

Over the next few days, other family members such as aunts, uncles and cousins would come to visit and check in to see how my initial recovery was progressing. It was great to feel the love and support as each person gave me a kiss on the cheek or a light hug with the focus of not coming close to the impacted area. It was nice to see familiar faces and hear their words of endearment. As each member of my family came to visit, it gave me a little more motivation to keep pushing and working towards recovery. I knew the road would be long and difficult, pushing me to give up at certain moments, but focusing on returning to my family and being as close to "normal" as possible was my goal. There was no compromise. I had to return.

It was later revealed to me, when my mother and the surgeon who had saved my life came to visit, that two-thirds of the total amount of blood in my entire body was in my stomach. I had come down with mono. That was resulting in the extreme levels of fatigue and causing my spleen to enlarge as a way of fighting off the infection, thus pushing my rib cage to protrude out over my inflated organs.

The impact from the on-ice collision had punctured a hole in my spleen, causing blood to slowly drip into my stomach. Once my stomach had filled up with enough blood, my body began to dry heave. The sheer force of my body trying to throw up caused my spleen to finally rupture. When this happened I lost feeling in my body, resulting in my head hitting the toilet in front of me. A person only has twenty-four hours to remove the ruptured spleen and the blood filling up the stomach before a person's body would completely shut down, resulting in death.

Once the ambulance had arrived at my home, they rushed me into the hospital for a quick evaluation by the surgeon to see where the source of the pain was coming from. The surgeon put pressure on my side and I began to cry out loud, howling from the excruciating pain. After briefly explaining the procedure to my parents at 1:00 AM, the hospital staff quickly rushed me into the emergency room and began pumping more pain relieving drug into my body and began surgery to remove my ruptured spleen, empty the blood that had filled up almost my entire stomach, and then quickly worked on controlling the bleeding that could have flooded and damaged other vital organs. The surgery lasted for two hours where the time of completion was 3:00 AM. Over twenty staples were used to close the wound and prevent from any infection. Needless to say, I am extremely lucky and blessed to have such great people and God looking over me in these moments.

After all of the family members had come and gone, I knew the real work would begin. It would be challenging, but failure was not an option. I needed to get my life back and I needed to prove to myself that I could complete the strenuous process towards recovery.

The difficult rehabilitation tests first included building up my lungs and stomach through breathing exercises, one of which included a small machine called a Spirometer. I had to blow into a large plastic tube that contained a blue plastic ball inside, and the ball would hover up and down based on the strength of my exhales. The importance of this exercise was to keep my lungs inflated, strengthened, and (most importantly) prevent pneumonia.

At first I could barely get the ball to come off the ground, as the pain in my stomach flowing up to my chest and lungs was too much to continue. I could feel the burning sensation in my lungs, quickly flowing up my throat. The pressure and rawness of the exercise caused me to cough with regularity, resulting in drinking large amounts of water as the exercise would dry my mouth and throat. Over the next couple weeks and after several attempts, I would build up my lungs to the point where I could keep the ball safely hovering over the blue line that was painted on the tube. Test one was complete!

The next rehabilitation test was for me to build up enough strength to be able to walk down the hospital hall holding onto the heart machine and returning safely to the onlooking nurse. At first, just getting up was considered a success, as the blood would quickly flow from my extremities to my face, throwing off my balance and equilibrium, and forcing me to return to the hospital bed that had become my safety net. After a month of slow progress, building one step at a time, the trip to and from my room was accomplished. Test two was complete!

Now onto the final test, which was composed of two criteria. The first part was to let my stomach heal from all the trauma and strengthen my core enough to eat solid food—enough food that I could keep it down and allow it to pass through my body. The second and final part of the test was that I needed to show the nurse this crucial "evidence." My first attempts to keep food down failed, but I was eventually able to hold down green beans. Now I just needed one thing: feces. I needed to return home, to normalcy. My salvation finally came on Salisbury steak day. Though the nurse was far from impressed, I was ready to go.

"Call my parents," I shouted. "I'm ready to go home, now!"

"Alright, alright sir," the nurse replied as she slowly walked out of the room tapping her fingers against the plastic clipboard she was holding.

I remember saying one word over and over again as I lay on the tiled floor, with sweat dripping down my face knowing the hardest part was over: "Yes!" The road to recovery would leave the Buffalo City Hospital, and now continue in the familiar confines of Oakridge Drive, located in the quiet suburb of Hamburg.

When I returned home to stay with my family, I would continue my daily routine of breathing exercises, taking walks around the house and up and down stairs, and gradually consuming solid food for all three meals. As I started to gain more strength, I would test limits by walking further and unsupervised. After three months of this strict regime, I started to gain some weight back, but the big test was soon to come. After I started walking, which turned into light jogging, it was time to attempt a light aerobic workout.

The first time was miserable. I spent more time coughing and taking breaks than actually exercising. This was a huge blow to my confidence. Once easily-performed exercises were now almost impossible to accomplish. It was very difficult to take as I take pride in my workouts, consistently trying to push a little more than before. I had lost twenty pounds through the surgery and recovery process, down to a mere 170 pounds on my six-foot one-inch frame.

Slowly, I continued to build every other day, until I could complete my Insanity workout videos like before. First it was running in place, then it was jumping up and down which evolved into light squats and pushups, then came more challenging exercises like burpees. Rebuilding my strength, especially in my chest and core, was excruciating, but I'm extremely grateful for the opportunity, as the expected outcome going into surgery could have been much worse.

Going through this process, first and foremost, I realized how fragile life truly is. It can be taken for granted and then stripped away in a moment's notice. I realized how important family and close friends are throughout the process of recovery, as sometimes you need others to help motivate you through difficult times.

In light of the difficulty of my recovery, it is extremely important here to mention one person who spent several days by my side, helping me through the mental aspect of long rehabilitation, and keeping me focused on the next task. That person was my mother's younger

41

sister, Aunt Cynthia.

At the time, she had four children of her own at home that she was responsible for, but she stayed day in and day out to help see me through this ordeal. It would be a lack of respect and gratitude if I did not mention her at this stage. There were very tough and dark days when I wanted to give up and accept that it was going to be too hard for me to recover, but she was strong enough for the both of us. I owe her a lot for getting me through, providing me hope, and encouraging me to keep pushing onward. Whenever I would get down or get depressed about how long the recovery was, she was right there to say, "You have great and loving parents, sister, and family who are looking forward to you coming home, don't disappoint them" or "Don't worry how long it'll take, what's the next task we have to work on for today?"

Every time I see my aunt, I make it a point to go straight up to her, kiss her on the cheek and say "I love you," because she knows where that is coming from and that there is a deeper meaning behind those words. I am grateful to have her in my life and by my side during the long process.

Most importantly, I started to learn how important my faith in things I couldn't see or understand and my relationship with God was. I had little faith before this event occurred; I took things and people for granted. I didn't reciprocate acts of kindness. I took and took and took but never gave back. I had no right to act privileged and expect people that cared so much, to take care of me. I took advantage of people that loved me for granted because I abused their unconditional love.

In short, I was an ungrateful punk. Sitting in the hospital bed and back at home in Hamburg, I realized how difficult this life can be if you don't trust your instincts and know when you've hit your limits. It almost cost me my life, but my faith in people and in God was on full display through this ordeal and I became a better person because of it.

Chapter 3:
Alcohol and Grandparents' Passing

"Your past mistakes are meant to guide you, not define you."

-Author Ziad K. Abdelnour

After the long and strenuous road to recovery was complete, I was able to finish my last college semester and graduate with honors from SUNY Fredonia with a degree in Accounting. I would find and hold down an auditing position at a large local firm named Johnson and Sanders in Buffalo. I had found a career in my field and worked in what I thought I wanted over the next three years, but I wasn't happy; I wasn't inspired by the work I was doing.

I wasn't changing the world. I was completing the same routine tasks over and over again for small time clients. I wanted more, but was never given the opportunity by my supervisor. I wanted to make a bigger impact for larger clients, but was ignored or pushed aside when my requests were presented. I wanted to be in the larger downtown office where all the people my age were. I wanted to become part of that group, but was put into the smaller office in East Aurora.

I was miserable with the way my career had started out and needed a change, but couldn't find a way to be happy. I was sad and angry at the world for taking my grandfather away from me. I had been through enough. It wasn't right; it wasn't fair. I was spiraling out of control. I let people around me influence me to drink on a regular basis. They used it for fun—I used it to mask the pain and the failure I had become.

I failed my grandfather.

I wasn't living up to my promise. I needed to be better, but was drowning in guilt and reaching out to alcohol as a life preserver. I was in my early twenties, but I was killing my body. I looked and felt older than the people in my group. That's what alcohol does. It tears you down, it takes everything, and gives you nothing in return. It's a silent friend who is there to listen, but doesn't offer any guidance on how to help. It takes unmercifully and offers only a short term fix, but never a long term solution. I missed my grandparents, and I would dream of them, trying to bring them back into my reality.

My grandfather, Michele (pronounced Mee-kehleh) Agostini, born in 1919 from Racalmuto, Sicily, was the youngest of ten children. His father was a policeman and came from a hardworking lower middle class family. He was about thirty-one years old when he left "the old country" in 1950 as it became too corrupt and dangerous. He was also strongly urged by his sister Concetta to leave and join her in North America, as he needed to start a new life for himself and had relatives whose last name was Martorelli living in Hamilton, Ontario, two hours outside of Toronto.

An interesting fact is that my grandfather's mother, Teresa Martorelli, was first cousins with Gaetano Martorelli. Gaetano's son Rosario and my grandfather Michele were close cousins. Rosario's sons, Robert and Tommy Martorelli, along with my father Patrick and my Uncles Louis and Michael have remained extremely close to this day. Their children and my cousins and I are still close to this day. That's four generations of Martorelli's and Agostini's that directly go back to the little town of Racalmuto, Sicily. That's a special relationship that will continue to grow and strengthen well into the next generation.

Tommy and Robert Martorelli are the brothers that I never had. I speak to them on a regular basis, sharing these stories because I could confide in them. We would consistently catch up and visit one another. They are brothers I can rely on for any type of life advice, from career to relationship. They have known me my entire life, even when I was a little boy of no more than five, running in their parents' flower or vegetable garden.

Going to visit them and their parents, Rosario and Lucia, was always special. I would hear stories about my grandfather and the close relationship they all had. I would hear the stories of how they would visit one another and have big dinners in Buffalo and Hamilton. Being in Hamilton, Ontario is like visiting Italy: hearing the beautiful romance language being spoken by adults being passed down to their children; the Roman architecture filling the inside of their homes; and of course the delicious food, such as spaghetti with Bolognese sauce paired with a full bodied cabernet, followed by espresso with a cannoli or éclair for dessert. It is great to be in the same place where my family began, the place my grandfather made his home in North America. Sometimes I wonder what life would have been like if he stayed in Racalmuto. If he raised a family there, how different my life would have been!

My grandfather came to North America through the port of Nova Scotia, as immigration to the United States was closed at that time. Since Canada was only

48

accepting farmers, and my grandfather being a tailor, he strategically had "agriculture" written as his occupation on his passport. The funny story my grandfather would always tell Rosario and their friends down on James Street, was when he was at Immigration and the Security Officers examined him as he went through Customs. When asked if he was a farmer, he smartly said yes. The officer examined his manicured and non-callused hands, questioning what farming or hard labor he had ever done. Intelligently, he replied by saying he was a supervisor of the farmers. Luckily for my family, he was passed through Canada as a farmer. Within weeks, my grandfather worked at a local tailor shop where he continued to hone his craft and would later start his own tailoring business in Buffalo called Mike's Tailor Shop. He was the first person in our family to start his own business.

My grandmother, Mary, born in in 1926 in Pitson, Pennsylvania, was the youngest of three. Her father was a coal miner. She enjoyed music and dancing, like most girls her age, and was always looking for the perfect man to call her husband. She loved to order QVC or through the Sears Catalogue for herself, and would spoil her grandchildren to no end. Her grandchildren are what she lived for.

My grandparents met at the Fort Erie Italian club

in Canada and were introduced by my grandfather's sister Concetta. In 1953, my grandparents moved to and were married in Buffalo, NY. The rest was history. They would be married for fifty years while giving birth to three boys and having several grandchildren who adored them.

My grandfather passed away in November of 2002 due to pancreatic cancer, exactly one year and two days before I would have my emergency spleen surgery. My grandmother passed away in August 2004 due to heart conditions and emphysema. They had lives full of happiness and great memories that were spent with family. We should all be that lucky.

My grandparents were wonderful to me and my sister. They would do anything to make us happy. They took care of us like we were their own children and made us feel special every time we would visit. It was always fun going to grandma and grandpa's house when they would watch us, while our parents were both away working. Monday through Friday we would get there at 7 AM on the dot.

It would be painful getting up so early in the morning—around 6 AM—when my mom, sister, and I would pile into the blue station wagon half asleep. I would be exhausted and grouchy, and would immediately fall asleep during the thirty minute drive from Hamburg into the city of Buffalo. Once my head hit the back of the car seat, I was out. By the time we would pull into the driveway on Busti Avenue, my eyes would just start to open as the sun would start to rise, glaring across my face to announce the start of a new day.

I would patiently wait for my mom to come over to unbuckle me from the car seat. Once she picked me up and my Nike sneakers hit the ground, I was off. I would fly around the blue station wagon, up the three small steps, and straight into the kitchen where my grand-mother would be cooking my special breakfast. I would fly right into her awaiting arms and she would pick me up to eye level, while I could hear the kielbasa cooking in the frying pan. I'll always remember the smell of the sausage aroma consuming the room. She would give me tiny little kisses on my right cheek then bring me over to the toaster. It was like clockwork.

By the time she directed us to the left, in front of the toaster, the frosted, sugar-filled Pop Tarts would spring up to meet us. It probably wasn't the healthiest of breakfasts, but it was my staple, every day, for as far back as I could remember. She would put the sausage and Pop Tarts in the famous blue dish that was strictly for me and I would sit in her lap swinging my legs, waiting for her to finish cutting my food. Once she was done, I would get another quick kiss and then barreled into the living room where my cartoons were awaiting me. I would watch the always popular "Smurfs" and ate like a king while watching my favorite program. My sister would be off doing God knows what, as she was too mature for such baby shows. Her loss.

I had the whole room to myself as I would throw myself into the brown Barcalounger that was my grandpa's chair. No one sat in his chair, except for his only grandson, but when I would hear him come downstairs, his perfectly shined dress shoes clapping against the linoleum of the kitchen floor, I knew he was near. I would turn to my left and see the perfectly dressed tailor ready to start his day. He always had on beautiful blue, black, or grey suits with his blue eyes staring into mine and his slicked back brown hair. He was an impressive sight.

"That's my chair!" he would declare, but slowly turn his serious face into a smile when he saw it was me. "I guess you can sit there while I go to work," he would say in the broken Italian/English dialect only a few could understand. I was in the special chair eating my ultra-healthy breakfast. I think that's where they came up with the phrase "breakfast of champions," but I could be mistaken. I was the king of the castle. He would give me a hug and would start his day, heading out the door towards the Ellicott Building where his tailor shop resided.

With every bite, I could feel my body slowing down, closer and closer to a state of sound sleep. Hours would go by because when I would wake up my show wasn't on anymore. Instead, I would see some kind of soap opera displayed in my frontal view. What the heck was this? I would look towards the kitchen, as my grandma would be sitting at the kitchen table, with a big smile on her face while watching her "shows." Every once in a while, I would change the channel, just to get her going, but would quickly change it back when I heard her howl, "Hey, I'm watching that!"

Once the show was done, I would act as her human remote control, going channel by channel looking back for her approval if the current channel would suffice. A simple nodding or shaking of her head would let me know. Right before I would have enough, she would find the channel that she liked. Most of the time it was the local news.

That was my cue to go outside and see what my sister was up to. When I would go outside towards the three panel garage door, I would usually see her in the driveway playing with a doll or with a neighbor. Either way, I didn't exist to her. No matter; I got used to the special treatment being the little brother. I would learn to make my own fun by either picking the flowers that grew on the large fence or running over to the large barrel where my grandfather kept his basil plants. I would either play with the dirt that surrounded the basil plants or water them, but one thing was certain: I loved smelling them. The potent aroma was pleasant to my nose. To this day, when I smell basil in a pasta dish, I will close my eyes and it takes me back to those special summer days at my grandparent's house. I would pick a couple pieces of basil, run back into the kitchen and hand them to grandma, as she would use them in the perfectly blended pasta sauce that she and I would eat for a late lunch or dinner before my mom would arrive to pick us up.

Once or twice a week the afternoon schedule would differ, as my grandma would take us to different restaurants or establishments such Rich's Bakery store on Niagara Street for fresh bread and pastries. When my family and I reminisce, my favorite story is always the trip to Rich's. We would leave the house on Busti Avenue and head to Niagara Street. In reality, these streets were parallel to each other and no more than two miles away, but the trip would literally take us two hours to arrive at our destination, since my grandma wouldn't drive above ten miles per hour and constantly stop every ten feet to let trailing cars that "were in such a hurry" pass us by.

We would begin at my grandma's blue two-story house on Busti Avenue; my sister and I would sit in the back seat of the grey Buick, while our grandma sat in the front. She didn't have car seats that I can recall, so neither my sister nor I could see above the window. We would have no idea where the car was on the street or what landmarks we were passing. She would pull the car out of the garage then get out and slowly walk towards the garage door to close it, then slowly return to the car. Then she would begin to perform several three point turns, back and forth, back and forth, until she wiggled the Buick in the right direction so she could drive out of the driveway going straight. This was necessary for her as the driveway was too narrow for her to back out of. Then she would wait for all the cars on the street to pass then slowly making her right onto the main street.

All I can remember is seeing the tops of cars fly by us as we inched down the street. After what felt like and literally was eternity, the car would abruptly stop, and she would turn off the engine and turn back to us and say, "Okay, we're here!"

Jokingly, my sister and I would look at each other in bewilderment, wondering where the heck "here" was. We would have believed Rich's bakery was in Canada, and not in the United States, as the Canadian border was within 10 miles of Busti Avenue and considering the time it took to arrive. Other favorite spots were Ted's hotdogs, and the small custard shop for ice cream as dessert. These were funny yet unforgettable moments of my childhood. What I would give to be back in that Buick with my grandmother! How often I wish for that trip to take longer, so I could spend more time with her. I would give anything to turn back the hands of time to those summers in downtown Buffalo.

As time went by, my sister would go off to kindergarten, eventually leaving just me with my grandmother. I would sit at the large kitchen table, suitable for ten to twelve people, and watch my grandmother as she made pasta sauce. My grandma, who stood five feet six inches tall and had curly black hair, always wore colorful dresses as she cooked. I would always stand on the chair next to the stove to get a closer view. I would watch her put in the whole tomatoes, the sugar or milk to lessen the acidity of the sauce, salt, pepper, and finally I would add my touch: the basil.

It was fun to watch her cook, as anything worth doing well is usually a lengthy process. Our family could eat her cooking for days. She would make spaghetti with meatballs, spare ribs, spicy sausage and put them all into the sauce to cook. Sometimes she would make raviolis during the day, just for me, as a reward for being her "little helper." She would ask me what I wanted and my answer was always raviolis. She took her time and mastered her craft.

I would sit at the kitchen table, as the smell of the sauce wafted into my nostrils. Once the sauce was ready, she would boil the raviolis for a couple minutes and then put them on my special blue plate and added the sauce, olive oil, a small piece of bread, and lastly, some parmesan cheese to top it off. It was perfection. As I shoveled the food into my mouth, she would tell me to take my time, and enjoy tasting the different ingredients that were on my plate.

That's where my love affair with Italian food started. I loved the basil, the extra virgin olive oil, and the ricotta cheese that filled the ravioli. The best part, however, was the sauce. Grandma would just sit and smile, appreciating how I always cleaned the entire plate with the piece of Italian bread, usually asking for more. She would never give me extra as she would say it would spoil my dinner, and over time she instilled that patience and that discipline within me.

She enjoyed taking care of her family, and especially her only grandson. We had a special bond between us that strengthened over those summer days, before I went off to start kindergarten. I appreciate everything she did for me. She was a great listener as I would tell her about my favorite television shows, colors, and having her son Patrick as my father. Whenever I have a plate of raviolis at a restaurant—though they are never quite as perfect as what she would make me—the dish takes me back to my childhood and the one on one time I spent with her.

It wouldn't be too long after my raviolis before my grandfather would come home from work, pull up a chair next to me, and prepare for dinner. At the dinner table, I would usually be scribbling in my coloring book, while he put the napkin in his collar and filled up his glass of Lake Country red wine from a huge glass jug. Next, he would put the fork in his right hand, the spoon for twirling his pasta in the left hand, and impatiently wait for his dinner.

It was kind of funny to witness my grandma, as she would sometimes purposely go into the bathroom or into another room so he would eventually have to prepare his own meal. He wasn't happy about that, but after a couple sips of wine and spoonfuls of pasta, he was content. It was always nice of him to give me a sip of red wine before my grandma would come back into the kitchen; she always asked him if he had just done what she thought he did!

She didn't like him giving me wine, but at the age of six, I was old enough in his eyes to have a taste. I wasn't going to argue. He would always talk about how the wine blended with the sauce so beautifully as he kissed his fingers in a typical Italian gesture. When asked if he had given me wine, the two of us would look at each other with total confusion, then look back at her and simultaneously say "no." Then as she turned away, we would turn and give each other a small grin to verify we got away with it—but she knew, she always knew.

During the week the kitchen table was my domain. I would eat, color, and play with my toys at the table, but when the weekends came the grand table was for adults only. This was the table my parents, aunts, uncles, and grandparents would sit at for Sunday dinner at 1:00 PM sharp. Meanwhile, my sister and I would sit in the living room by ourselves to eat off of the TV trays. They would always close the glass door that separated the kitchen from the living room, so the noise would be contained.

There wasn't enough room for me, so I would always wonder what went on in the kitchen table. I never understood why I couldn't join them, as I spent more time in that room than any of them. I deserved to be there and not being allowed would upset me. I would hear glasses clanging and people laughing, but my name was not on the list.

Whenever I would gain enough courage to see what was happening, I would go next to one of my parents, asking for more food just so I could steal a few seconds of their time. They were always in the middle of a conversation or a great story, so once I had my new plate of pasta, I was quickly directed back outside the room where the silence was deafening. I never made it into that room, at that table, but sometimes I would pretend to be around all the older relatives. I would imagine discussing big plans, future vacations, and important business being handled. I was too young to understand the reason why I was kept away from the adults, but I knew I wanted to be there.

Instead, I would sit in silence until about 2:00 PM, when they all piled into the living room to watch the Buffalo Bills football game. No one wanted to eat with me, and now I was being pushed off of the chair so people could watch Jim Kelly lead the offense up and down the field in the early nineties. No respect, I tell you.

As time passed and I became a teenager, my family would still meet my relatives for Sunday dinner; that was great, as it was important to keep up traditions. As I continued to grow up and mature, everyone noticed how similar my grandfather and I looked alike, from our hair color and style, to our uncanny bright blue eyes, and even to the way we dressed. Everyone in the family has brown eyes except for us. It made me feel special being different while sharing a trait that was passed down directly from him. I always enjoyed dressing up with my finest clothes when I saw my grandparents. It was always a special event seeing them for dinner. I wanted to carry myself the way my grandfather did.

My relatives, the Martorellis, from Hamilton, friends of theirs, and even strangers in the neighborhood would see us together and state the similarities. It was nice to be recognized by everyone. I was seen as an adult when I was with him or when I would be introduced by him. People would see me and immediately start telling me stories of weddings and past times as if I were him.

Over time, I began to acquire those stories and make them my own. In the beginning it was great, but over the years as I got older, it wasn't fun anymore. It hit me hard the night he passed away at the age of eighty-two. I remember going to his funeral—the first one I had ever been to—and being scared, extremely lost, and overwhelmed.

I had never seen a person laying in a coffin before. All the blood was drained out of his body. It was scary feeling his legs and feeling nothing but the bone. I was afraid to touch his cold hands. This didn't look like the man I grew up with; his body was cold and his face sunken in. It was too much for me to process at the age of fifteen. I was grown up by age, but was not mature enough to handle the circumstances.

When it became too much, I went up to my friend Anthony's mother, who I had known well, and began sobbing. I couldn't hold in the sadness and the pain anymore. I needed to let it out. After his death, I felt lost. I had grown so accustomed to him being there for me to spend time with and talk to me about life.

There was only one big problem. I was named after, and very closely resembled, a man that I had come to adore. I lived off his memory and off his experiences. I was carrying on the end of his life, preserving his memory, and living in his shadow. I never carved out an identity or a life's purpose for myself.

I felt that when he passed away, he was taking me with him. I was dying inside and didn't know how to make it stop. Short-term happiness was quickly taken away with sorrow and depression. I couldn't make it stop, it was bigger and stronger than me. My struggle went on for two years—the worst two years of my life. My alcohol abuse continued further the day my grandmother went

into the hospital because she was having trouble breathing and had fallen. Her weight was too much to bear, so
she became bed ridden. Her breathing would continue
to hinder her until the point that she depended on an
oxygen tank for assistance.

I remember one day in particular, when I had gone
to visit her at the hospital. When I got off of the elevator,
I saw a group of ten to fifteen residents that were sitting
there watching television, which could have been the
show "Family Feud" on at the time. I quickly walked past
them to go visit my grandmother. I remember walking
faster than normal and with urgency.

When I found her room and made the right into
the door frame, all I could see was emptiness. The bed
was made, but she wasn't there. I checked the bathroom,
not there. What could have happened? Did her breathing condition get worse? I quickly walked back towards
the group of seniors and the nurses' station across from
them. Before I could ask them where my grandmother
Mary was, I remember something pulling my focus to
the right, away from the nursing staff and into the backs
of the heads of the residents watching television. Why
was I focused on them? What was attracting my attention
there?

All I could see was the backs of heads, one by one,

until I saw a pair of the most frightened eyes looking back at me. These eyes jumped out at me, startling like a shovel to the head. It was my grandmother. It almost knocked me off my feet. I had never seen her like this— so scared, so frightened, so helpless. I didn't know what to do. My mind was spinning. I couldn't focus. I was afraid to go near my own grandmother; the one who had taken care of me, the one who had watched me every day while my parents were at work, the one who would take me out for Ted's hotdogs and got me ice cream during the summer months, the most cherished and happiest days of my childhood. I was afraid. I couldn't approach her. I tear up just thinking about that moment. She needed me to be there, she needed me to take care of her, but I didn't know how. I froze. It was too much for a 19-year-old to handle. or maybe it was just too much for me.

I finally composed myself after what had been a frantic few moments, grabbed her wheelchair, and quick-ly guided her into her room. I turned her around so she could focus on me.

"What is wrong? I asked. "What happened? You're scaring me." She was still frightened; her eyes rapidly moving back and forth. Why was she like this? This wasn't her. Something had to be wrong.

She kept saying to me, "Take me home, why won't

you take me home? Don't you love me? I won't take up much room, I promise. Am I going to die?" She would start to cry when I told her everything was alright, as she told me I was lying to her. It was crushing me to see her like this. What was happening?

I knew this feeling as I had seen it in myself during the final moments before surgery. She was hallucinating. Did she take her necessary medication? Did she take too much? Was she having trouble breathing? I quickly ran my fingers along the tube that was inserted into her nostrils and ran them down towards the green oxygen tank. As I got towards the end....bingo! The tube was detached from the tank. She wasn't getting air. I quickly attached the tube to the tank and then checked to see if that had any effect. I focused on her eyes to notice any change.

After a minute or two, the longest of my life, her bloodshot eyes had started to de-strain and return to normal. She closed her eyes and continued to focus on her breathing. I ran to tell the nurse what had happened, yelling about how they could let this happen, as we returned back to my grandmother's room.

As the nurse was helping secure the tube, I asked my grandmother, "Are you okay now, are you getting air?" Her blood shot eyes opened and she gave me a little nod. I went over to her and kissed her cheek three little times, as I had always done and she had done to me, saying, "Don't scare me like that ever again." She had a blank stare on her face as if she had no idea what had just occurred.

I returned home, continuing to gather myself, but then later broke down in front of my mother while telling her what had happened. I never felt so helpless, so afraid in my life. I didn't want to be consoled. I wanted to be left alone. I wanted to wallow in my anger with the world. That was the last time I ever saw my grandmother alive. She passed away that night. I never got to tell her I loved her, I never got to tell her I understood why she acted that way, and more damaging, I never got to say goodbye. It still haunts me until this day, as I wipe the tears off of my keyboard now.

There have been times that I have had vivid dreams of my grandparents, so real and so strong that I would wake up in a cold sweat. I believe that loved ones who have passed find a way to reach out to us to see how things are or to express a feeling or thought to certain people within their family. It's their way to check in with the living, and to let them know that their spirit lives on.

In my case, I have had one vivid and life-like dream with each grandparent. These dreams were so real that I would wake up and stare at the ceiling in amazement, quickly analyzing every second of the encounter for clues on its meaning.

It was over five years after my grandfather passed when I had a brief but powerful dream encounter. In my dream, I remember being back at my grandparents' home, walking up the steps like I used to when I was a little boy. I walked into the kitchen, but instead of running into my grandmother's arms, the kitchen was dark and desolate. My grandmother was not by the kitchen stove, like I had seen thousands of times before. In fact, the entire house was dark.

As I walked from the kitchen towards the living room, in the direction of my grandfather's chair, I walked past the small room to the right where my grandfather would tailor clothes. The "sewing room" consisted of a small sewing machine that rested upon a wooden table and in front of a small wooden chair, a single closet where he would hang up the finished clothes, and last but not least, a single small lightbulb in the corner that hung from the ceiling.

As I walked past the sewing room I noticed the room was not dark like the rest of the house, but in fact a deep florescent red color. It was such a dark and rich red that it quickly reminded me of blood—the same red that I had seen drenching the mound of towels that I saw after my surgery, when I had abruptly woken up.

I walked into the small room and looked up at the hanging red lightbulb that was swaying back and forth. Turning my head to the right, I was startled to see my grandfather sitting on the table next to the sewing machine with his feet on the seat of the chair. He had on a simple undershirt and pants, with his head resting on top of his hands. Once he saw me, he rose up to greet me with a kind smile.

He was so much younger than I ever remember him being. He had a full head of thick brown hair that was slicked back. He couldn't have been more than thirty years old at the time. It was unreal. I knew who he was and he immediately knew me without any question. After exchanging pleasantries, he asked me how I was and how the family was doing. I told him I was good, still playing hockey at a high level, and that the family was doing well and was happy. I told him we all missed him and still thought about him.

He quickly responded with a smile and said, "That's good, I'm happy things are good, I have to go now." I urged him to stay, but he refused, stating that he needed to leave. He looked me in the eyes, then I instantly woke up in bed, flustered from what I just witnessed.

I remember every word and every detail. I have

never been able to create this vivid interaction again. I've tried countless times to recreate the moment and have even pleaded with him in my thoughts to talk with me, but to this day, he has never come back. He has moved on to heaven. I miss him and I know he's looking down even though I can't hear his voice in my mind anymore. Time has taken his voice from me, but I know he's happy.

The dream I had with my grandmother was a little more peculiar. There was the same beginning of the dream encounter with me walking up the stairs and into the kitchen, with the room being dark. This time, however, my grandmother was sitting at the kitchen table like she used to while I turned the television channels for her from the living room. I sat down and said hello. She smiled, but it quickly faded to a concerned look. I asked her what was wrong.

She responded, "How come you don't visit me anymore, you don't stop by the house like you used to?" I was so confused. How could I visit her? I told her I loved visiting her, but she quickly interrupted me by asking, "Why haven't you or the family visited me?"

I responded back, "We do visit you at the cemetery all the time, what do you mean?" The moment I said the word "cemetery" her eyes looked to the floor in con-fusion and bewilderment, as I could see her mind was running wild.

"Cemetery? Why would you visit me at the cemetery?" she asked. I began to rub my neck with my hand and cleared my throat. I had no idea how to tell her.

Finally I replied, "We go to the cemetery because you're no longer with us grandma. I'm sorry." She immediately looked sad and confused, trying to fully process what I had just told her, then she was gone.

I felt so puzzled waking up from the encounter. How did she not know? Was she in purgatory? It was unsettling to say the least, but I never heard back. I hope and pray that she found peace and made her way to heaven. I believe she has. Just like my grandfather, I was never able to recreate the moment again. It was sad to think about not being able to visualize a conversation with them anymore, as it has been over 15 years since either was alive, but I have learned to be okay with this as the years have passed.

At this point, my life was spinning out of control. Between the drinking and the unexpected deaths of my grandparents that I had admired and adored, I was scrambling. I had so many questions, but I had no answers. I was disgusted with the world, and used alcohol to further damage myself, along with pushing the ones I loved away, since I thought they were to blame.

I turned to anger as it was the only option I believed I had. I did not take accountability for my life. I had promised my grandparents, the foundation of our entire family, at their respective caskets that I would carry them with me throughout my life, but I was drowning with the weight I had been carrying. The quicker I moved my legs, the heavier the weight felt.

I needed to let them down off my shoulders and find a different perspective on life, but I struggled with this because I didn't want to feel I was forgetting or moving on without them. As a result of such guilt, I kept them on my shoulders when I should have been strong enough to put them down. My failure to move on would directly result in the worst decision I had made in my life.

It all came to a head in late August of that year. After a perfect season with my men's league hockey team being capped off with a 4-0 championship win, a few teammates and I went to a bar in Hamburg to celebrate. We had a section of the bar dedicated to our group where shots and mixed drinks of all different types were at our disposal. Let the great times roll!

We drank well into the early morning until the bouncers told us we had to leave. I felt I was okay to drive home because it was less than a mile away. I could do it, I just had to go straight.

I remember standing in front of the door with the keys in my hand and thought for a second, "Should I do this?" This thought was quickly washed away with supreme confidence, as I opened the door and pulled out of the parking lot. I made the right in my new V6 Silver Honda Accord and started heading towards home. I pulled up to the main intersection. All I had to do was go straight. Just go home, there was nothing out there for me.

Absolutely nothing…except food. I was hungry and it would help soak up all the alcohol that I had consumed earlier in the night. So I foolishly made the right and headed towards McDonalds. I turned up the music and coasted down the street for my late night meal. I pulled into the entrance and made my way to the back of the store. I pulled around to where the drive through menu was to start placing my order and looked ahead at the only other car that was in the parking lot at that hour. It was a police car.

My heart sank, and I knew I had made a horrible decision, but what could I do at this point? I had to proceed. I picked up my food and made my way to the exit and back onto the main road. I was fine and was okay. Then I saw the cop pull out behind me.

I told myself that it was alright; he was just going to follow me for a while then proceed down another street. I just had to stay straight and I was going to be fine. A few seconds later, the police lights went on. My mind raced as I knew what the end result would be. I pulled to the side towards the curb and waited. This had to be the most nervous I had been in my life.

As the police officer drew near, the blood rushed to my head, and my white knuckled hands clenched the steering wheel. He didn't even wait to ask for license and registration; he could smell the alcohol coming through the pores of my forehead, neck, and hands. "How much have you had son?" he asked, knowing full well it was more than the "couple" I had reiterated after being asked on a few occasions.

He asked me to repeat the alphabet. I went slowly then sped up at the end to get the process over with. I recall slurring a couple letters together, but no harm done. I don't think he noticed. Then he asked me to repeat the hand movements such as thumb to index finger, thumb to middle finger, and so on. I went slowly to make sure I got this part right.

Then the dreaded last request. "I am going to administer a breathalyzer test, are you going to comply?" I knew I couldn't do that, as there was no way I would stay under the legal limit.

My best option was to refuse. He asked again and I refused. I couldn't provide them the verification of what was already known. I couldn't have it documented on what my actual number was in that state of mind. My head continued to spin, but I wasn't truly and mentally there.

After a few moments, I was instructed to get out of the car, arrested, and placed in the back of the police patrol car. Reality hit me like a ton of bricks. How could this happen? I was given a second chance at life, to make a difference for not only myself, but for others, and this is what I do?

I squandered the opportunity I was given, and now I sat on the black leather seat looking through the metal fence that separated myself from the police officers in the front. I just sat in horror, watching my new car, being put onto a flatbed headed to the city impound.

I didn't even consider what I would have to say to my parents, and how I would explain this. I just wallowed in my own self-pity as we headed to the police station. When we arrived at the precinct, they directed me to a long wooden bench with one handcuff around my wrist and the other end secured to one of the rings attached to the bench. The officer tossed the McDonald's bag in my direction where it rested near my secured wrist.

"Eat up, you're going to be here for a while," said the officer as he started to file the paperwork. I just kept replaying the events in my head: if I had just driven straight, everything would have been different. Did the burgers mean that much, based on what they had just cost me? I couldn't even look up at the long vertical mirror in front of me. I was so disgusted with myself.

After being charged with Driving While Intoxicated, it was time for fingerprints. Every time my finger was forced from the inkpad to the paper, I felt a little more of my life being taken away. This wasn't me and this couldn't be what I had become. I had too much talent and intelligence to be in this situation, yet a path of mistakes and lack of good judgement landed me here.

The police then called my parents to have them pick me up. I will always remember the look of sheer disgust pasted across their faces. They couldn't even find the words to express the disappointment and internal rage they were holding in. It was no use; the horrible judgement that placed me here was done. The silence is what I remember most about the car ride. Every few seconds, when one of them wanted to start a tirade of reprimanding remarks, the other would just reach over and shake their head, reiterating that it wasn't even worth it anymore. For the first time in my life, I wished I would have died on that emergency room table with my insides open for heaven and God to see.

This was it. There were no words to turn me around, no hope for a brighter future. The silence stuck into me like the scalpel did just a couple years back. I had no feeling left in me. No disappointment anymore, no frustration, nothing. My parents' looks said it all—they had given up on me. When I finally made it up the stairs with their help, I just laid there staring up at the ceiling as it spun around me.

Then abruptly, for a moment in that pitch black room, I saw my grandparents looking back at me. They were both crying, then they were gone. I tried to visualize them coming back, but couldn't recreate the moment. I tried to relax as the tears ran down my cheeks. Finally, my eyes closed. Silence.

I slept through most of the next day, as I woke up around 4 PM then went back to sleep after a glass of water. I didn't want to see anyone; I couldn't bear to discuss the matter today. The following day was my court date after my father had spent the morning finding a lawyer to represent me.

On the way to the court house, my father would just keep repeating, "They should just keep you there,

there's nothing left for me to say." Over and over it continued.

I finally mustered up enough courage to mutter "I'm sorry."

My father just looked at me with disgust. "Do you know what you're doing to me, your mother, and this family? Tighten up your tie, you're going to be late. I can't believe we're fucking doing this," he declared, as his voice started to rise.

After sitting still for an hour and a half at the court house on the cold wooden benches, it was my turn. I was so embarrassed to be there. I had to be instructed on the protocol constantly by the judge and lawyer because I had never been in trouble like this before: where to stand, how to act, and most importantly, to keep my mouth shut.

The disrespect showed on the lawyer's and judge's faces. I was seen as nothing more than trash in their eyes. Everything changes when this happens, as society turns its back on you. You're not worth people's time anymore. You are just in the way of everyone else.

As I stood there, the beads of sweat forming on my face, the judge started his statement.

"Well we know why you're here, don't we?" he started. "I can't begin to tell you how reckless, dangerous, and stupid this whole situation is. Not only did you put yourself in harm's way," his voice bolstered out, "you could have killed someone!"

My gut tightened up at these words knowing full well there was no chance of getting my sentence reduced. As we know, a DWI is a felony in the United States. My chance at any kind of a successful life was over. I could feel my heart racing, combined with a sense of hopelessness.

"You have been charged with DWI, how do you plea?" the judge continued.

My lawyer stated, "He pleads not guilty, your honor."

Immediately the judge shouted, "I'm talking to him, I want to hear him say it!"

I could barely get the words "not guilty" out of my mouth before he interrupted me.

"Why is that? You refused a breathalyzer test and the severity of your crime warrants this punishment, what do you have to say?"

The sweat began to flow more frequently now because I knew the major implications of my next answer. There was no time to let pride get in the way. I had a sudden surge of adrenaline in that moment, as I stated, "I've made a horrible decision your honor, one that I can't come back from, one that will take the rest of my life to repair if I have a DWI on my record. I've lost the respect of my family and I don't believe in myself anymore, but I need a chance at a real life your honor. I need a chance to make something of myself as I've wasted my life to this point. My life is slipping away and I don't know how to get it back. I don't know if I'll recover from this."

The tears started to roll down my face. That was it. I had no control, no say, in where my life would go at this point. I either had a chance to right a wrong and build towards a brighter future, or I would be buried under another major setback.

The judge's tone lightened immediately at my words. He took pity on me as the lawyer started to state the deaths of my grandparents and spleen surgery that had all occurred within the past few years. "You may have given up on yourself, but I'm not here to bury people and leave them for dead. You have been through a lot I see, and you will have a long road to recover, but I want to see you get there."

For the first time in years, I felt hopeful; I had finally been given a break after so many things had piled up to leave me for dead.

"I have decided to lower your charge to DUI and you will be required to go through counseling and alcoholics addiction meetings, where a therapist will deem if you have an alcohol dependency or not. If you pass these requirements, your charge will be reduced to a DUI. I have spoken to Captain Sullivan who vouches for your character. Do we have a deal?" the judge asked.

"Yes, your honor," I replied, finally with some life in my voice. I was confused leaving the court house. Captain Sullivan? I knew him and his son through hockey, but I never realized my father had reached out to him for a favor.

I will always be internally grateful and indebted to Captain Sullivan. He gave me another chance to turn things around. I would later stop by his office with my father to thank him for his assistance. We talked about when I was a little boy, so full of promise and talent to play hockey, and full of character.

His parting words will always remain with me: "How about that little boy that I remember when I first met you, so full of optimism and character, how about he returns? What I see now is not what I remember and that's disappointing." His words rang in my ears.

As I left his office, the feeling of relief washed over my body. I was given another chance at life, when honestly I don't know if I deserved one at the time. I knew there wouldn't be a third chance. This was it. This was the beginning again. Time to start living the life I was meant to live. There was a reason I was pulled from the depths of hell twice. There were bigger plans for me. I truly believed that at the time and I do now. I was spared to do something great with my life—an opportunity to do it right. I am not entitled, but grateful for the chance to turn things around. The road to recovery has begun.

CHAPTER 4:
RECOVERING

"Take the first step in faith. You don't have to see the
whole staircase. Just take the first step."
—Quote from Martin Luther King Jr.

The road to recovery can be long. It can wear on you, it will show you what you are made of, but it all starts with you. You are the orchestra conductor, and you are the pilot. The beautiful piece of music cannot begin to be shared with the world, nor can the immaculate white Leer Jet take off down the runway towards the cloudless sky, without these essential people being ready and confident enough to start their journey.

I would need to be that conductor, that pilot, in my own life. I needed to find the confidence, determination, and motivation that I once had in spades—the extreme confidence when I skated in front of the 2,000+ crowd in central New York, three years earlier, celebrating with my teammates and holding the State Championship Trophy in my arms. Thoughts of the work I had put in had filled my mind, along with the dedication that it took not only from myself, but from every teammate over the course of a three-year process culminating into this single moment of triumph.

I would need to get back to that and in a hurry. I would have to turn my life around before I endured another major setback, one that I could not come back from. The road would be long, but I believed that I would get there one day to the peak of my being, to the euphoria and internal peace that I had been searching for—no, destined for. One day I would lay in an Adirondack chair, in a five-star resort in Bora Bora, Tahiti, Bali, or some island near the Indian Ocean, overlooking a crystal clear blue ocean and endless sky, sitting next to the woman of my dreams, my wife, knowing that I was okay. I would know that the hell I had put myself and my family through was worth the journey. This would be my "dream scenario." What a wonderful story that would be! I couldn't wait to share my story to inspire others.

In my head, I formed my end goal, my purpose in this life: my personal creed. I thought to myself, "Okay this is the goal; don't *ever* forget the goal, *everyday* take one significant step or make one significant action, to work towards this end goal to that scene of utopia—my internal heaven." Every day, I would remind myself of this goal, so I would keep myself on track and be accountable for how my life would turn out from here and now. I wanted nothing more from this life, but to be a great person, husband and one day, an even better father.

My mind quickly snapped back into the here and now, to the present day. The process would begin with the rehabilitation needed to rejoin society. I first needed to speak with a counselor at the alcohol addiction center, which had been mandated by the judge earlier.

I had my initial screening interview, which addressed many personal questions about the frequency and quantity of my drinking, to see what the scope of my issue truly was. At the time, I consumed a drink four days out of the week that would consist of three to five drinks at each sitting.

My parents did not have a drinking problem, nor did anyone in my family, but I was cursed with this personal burden because of the external situations surrounding me. I didn't come from an abusive home, my parents were still married, and I came from an upper middle class family where my parents, my sister and I all had stable jobs. The counselor was at a loss for a reason that would have generated such a habit.

As I sat in the wooden chair in front of her, I could

see her frustration starting to build, so I softly said, "My grandparents have recently passed."

The lightbulb had been turned on, and she stated, "Ah, let's discuss that." Over the next week, we would meet for two hours a day where we would dive into the passing of my closest grandparents, my surgery, and the drinking experienced in college, which were all understandable reasons for a person in their early twenties to be experiencing this issue.

The main point taken out of this meeting was that I didn't have a full-fledged addiction, but I had abused alcohol because I didn't know how to handle the external situations that were impacting my life and make healthy decisions to change them. It all had to start with me, all the aspects, and how they were impacting my thoughts and feelings. I needed to keep the things that worked or brought me joy, and I needed to cut out the ones that didn't add value or were holding me back. It would be difficult, but I didn't have a choice; I needed to save myself.

Before I could start my own personal evaluation, I would be required to attend Saturday morning alcoholic abuse meetings for three months. Every Saturday, the class of 20-30 people ranging from early twenties to late 50s, lasted from 8am until noon. In the sessions, we would discuss many topics that included why we were there, the final event that had resulted in being mandated to attend the class, and what were the external events that led us down this path towards self-destruction.

As I sat there over the three months, I had not only learned more about my own story, but was touched, moved, and shocked by the stories of the other members in the class. For example, I had witnessed a woman in her mid-fifties who had been arrested for DWI three times over a span of 15 years. It was gut wrenching listening to her story of how she had lost a child, who had drowned in a swimming pool while she was hosting a pool party years prior. She had everything she wanted in her life: a loving husband, a beautiful daughter, a blossoming career. All in one moment it was taken away, her life spiraled out of control and she never quite got it back to normal.

It's sad to see where her life had taken her. She wanted to turn things around, and she would come to tears while telling her story "countless times." She was looking for a way out, a way to become "normal" again. Her husband had left after a few altercations, where arguments had started over one partner blaming the other for the loss of their child. She was fired from her job for alcohol related problems. My heart broke for her.

I realized how truly fragile this life is, and the pain some of us endure.

I never knew what had happened to this woman, but I hope she was able to come to peace with losing her child and could find her definition of "normalcy" in this life, without painfully abusing herself with alcohol.

Another story included a man who would wake up each morning and drink a fifth of Jack Daniels to get his day started, which the class initially thought was funny. It was less so when he started to dig deeper into his life and how as a child he grew up with an alcoholic and abusive father that led to having suicidal thoughts, alcohol addiction, and several failed relationships. It is sad to see people who depend on alcohol as a way out, when in reality it is only drowning them further. It's tough to sit there and listen to their story of how they were once happy and loving people, but were currently just a shell of their former selves, looking for answers.

I was one of those people. It's a dark and lonely place when you have to face things alone and head on. Too many times, people never make it out, never see the light of day again. They never regain a semblance of themselves. The addiction takes hold and doesn't stop until it consumes them whole. They bury themselves in self-pity and guilt, embarrassed to reach out to loved ones, until the hole is too deep.

I can empathize with people who have gone through this struggle. I believe society just casts us off as weak and broken individuals, to never be heard from again, burying us further into despair. We deserve to be saved, with a chance to prosper and regain ourselves. I am a living example of how a person can regain their composure and sense of self-worth, and show society that I was worth saving. I'm not afraid to go back and talk about these dark days to those who are still suffering, because it led me to the light of better days. Talking to others that have experienced similar situations helps heal the mind and soul, not only for the person receiving my message, but also for me to heal and put the past away as well.

Every recovering person I have met has had their drug or alcohol abuse result directly from a life-altering moment, alcoholic family history, or childhood tragedy. They had normal lives like most, until outside influences or external circumstances led them down this road of self-destruction.

Alcohol is the most commonly used addictive substance in the United States. There are 17.6 million people, one in every 12 adults, who suffer from alcohol abuse or dependence along with several million more who engage in risky or binge drinking patterns that could directly lead to alcohol problems. I feel it's about time someone who has gone through this process and came out a better person than when they arrived spoke up with the goal of inspiring others, instead of being ashamed and hiding the truth from the ones they loved.

One thing I noticed is that too many people that have made the successful transition never return to those groups and help the others who are trying to follow suit. They quickly try to move on, bury themselves in their current reality, and do not give back to the people still struggling and desperately looking for a path to take. I feel they have an obligation to repay the small anonymous groups that helped them along their journey. If they want to admit it or not, this part of their life directly resulted in where they are today.

It's sad and unfortunate, but I am not one of those people. I want to give back. I have held small group discussions at Alcoholics Anonymous meetings in New York, and am now looking to grow this out to more people in person through my story.

I was spared since I was not convicted of a DWI charge, but it didn't come without its financial and emotional consequences. In the end, after lawyers and court fees, along with re-entrance costs to get my license and rights back into Canada to see my family, the experience cost me ten thousand dollars.

If the financial burden wasn't enough, it didn't compare to the family events that I missed because of the mistake that I had made. I wasn't able to enter Canada for over seven years because of the country's laws forbidding me to see my family. I wasn't able to see my relatives, wasn't able to attend the wedding dinner for my cousin Robert or meet his newborn son when he came into this world, and—even more damaging—wasn't able to attend the funeral of his mother Lucia as I couldn't get clearance quick enough before the funeral date was set.

I was forbidden to visit the place that my grand-father had made a home for so many years where I had enjoyed so many great memories. If it wasn't for the un-derstanding of the Martorelli family to come and visit me in Buffalo, my relationship with them would surely have disintegrated over those years. It's an attribute to their character that we kept in close contact over that time span, and actually became closer since the ordeal.

As I walked out of the last class, the sun shining directly into my eyes, I declared that this fear of despair and hopelessness would not happen to me. I would be strong enough to turn my life around. I would become the best version of myself. This would not be how my story ended, but instead, where it would begin.

CHAPTER 5:
ROAD TO NEW YORK CITY

"Make a choice. Just decide, what it's going to be, who you're going to be, how you're going to do it, just decide. And from that point, the Universe is going to get out of your way."

–Will Smith

I had all this momentum and determination, but I didn't know how to channel it, or where to focus my energy. I knew some of the decisions I would make would not be easy, but as Jack Canfield, the multimillion copy-selling author of "The Success Principles," stated, "If you keep on doing what you've always done, you'll keep on getting what you've always gotten."

If I was going to get towards my goal, my "dream scenario," I was going to need further education. At the time, I only had an undergraduate accounting degree from SUNY Fredonia. I was going to need something better, something from a more well-recognized school.

I looked at where some of the successful relatives in my family went to school in Buffalo, and decided upon a private Catholic school: Canisius College.

Here, I would obtain my Master's in Finance while I worked at the large local accounting firm. The process would take two years, but it was well worth the investment, as I expanded my knowledge in analyzing financial statements and began to lay the foundation of understanding and analyzing commonly purchased financial securities such as equities, bonds, options, futures, and swaps.

I always had an interest in the stock market, but didn't understand what caused large fluctuations on a daily, quarterly, and yearly basis to the major indexes. I would finally put in the focus that I lacked in high school and in undergraduate college where I graduated with a 3.3 and 3.4 GPA.

Some may think that is good, but I had the ability to do better, and I only cheated myself by not accomplishing more when I was younger. I wouldn't have changed the experiences and opportunities that I had obtained by playing in prep high school hockey and four years of college hockey, but I needed to focus more during those times. I needed to be able to balance my passion for sports and my strong interest in finance to generate a more favorable outcome.

But the past is the past; there is no point dragging around regret, as this would do me no good if I was going to pull myself out of the six-foot hole I had created. The dirt had been piling up for years, but it wasn't high enough to cover my nose and mouth. I could still breathe. My life wasn't done yet. I would call the shots in my life from this point on. All I could do now was concentrate on the future and new goals that I had set for myself and sacrifice everything to make sure they materialized.

At the end of year two in the Graduate Business School, I walked away on graduation day with a 3.65 GPA in finance from a well-respected school and had gotten back my motivation to achieve more with my life. I would change careers from accounting to finance and move out of my parents' home for the last time, at the age of twenty-five. There was no going back; I needed to learn how to be independent. I needed to see if the confidence I had gained was real.

I needed to put my progress to the test. In short, I needed to stand on my own two feet. I applied and accepted a Product Control Profit and Loss (PnL) mid-level position at Citibank in Buffalo. Here, I would combine my knowledge of financial analysis, along with financial products from graduate school, and use real working experience that I could build off of. I didn't start off making much money, but the point was to get working experience and continue to build off of the Master's Degree I obtained.

I will always remember my first day of work, before I had officially moved into my apartment and had a thirty five minute commute from the Southtowns of Hamburg to the Northtowns of Amherst. I started at 8 AM for a three-hour orientation that was discussing the company culture, filling out tax form information, and learning the overall lay of the land within the large, six-story complex at Cross Point Business Park, located in Getzville.

After the orientation had ended at 11 AM, as I made my way out of the large conference room, I was quickly approached by a female assistant. "You have an 11 AM meeting with Mr. Brown!"

As it was my first few hours at Citi, I had no idea who Mr. Brown was. The assistant quickly guided me to the 3rd floor and rushed me into a conference room and closed the door. I was completely caught off guard. One moment I was getting ready to begin another orientation seminar, and the next I am meeting with a person I didn't know, who apparently is very important. After a few minutes, the door flung open and in came a shorter man with a dark blue suit, flashy red tie, and jet black hair.

"Hello," he greeted me with his strong British accent, "I am Mathew Brown, the Managing Director of the Citigroup Financial Office here in Buffalo." He sat down across from me and quickly folded his arms as if he were trying to read my mind, like he was in a high stakes poker tournament.

After a couple of agonizing moments where he visually sized me up, having one eyebrow raised, then lowered, he opened his mouth and said, "Work hard and you'll do well here." He stood up, buttoned his blue suit coat, and headed towards the door.

I couldn't believe what I had just witnessed. Was this it? What do I do now? As his hand gripped the gold door knob of the conference room door, he turned back and asked, "You ever been to New York City mate?"

Taken aback by the strange delivery of the question, I replied, "No, I haven't, sir."

He grinned, as if he had heard the answer he was looking for. "Great. Well you've got a flight there at 3:30 PM this afternoon! Don't you bloody miss it!" Before I could even get the word "What" out of my gaping mouth, he had left the conference room and his assistant had quickly taken his seat directly in front of me, at the long rectangle conference room table.

The female assistant handed me a manila folder that included my boarding pass, flight itinerary, hotel information, and my boss's contact information.

As she started to get up, I stopped her abruptly, saying, "What are you talking about? Why am I going to New York City? For how long?"

She quickly shot back, "For job training, because that's where your boss and colleagues are, and for six months. Anything else?"

"Six months!!" I shouted.

"Yes," she replied. "You had better hurry, you only have four hours until your flight leaves! Go!"

I quickly grabbed my things as it was 11:15 AM and I still needed to drive all the way back home, pack my things, and head back where I came from to catch the 3:30 PM flight to JFK airport. I sprinted to my car with my folder tightly pressed under one arm, and a cell phone held in the other, quickly dialing my mother to throw all my business clothes into a suit case, along with all the toiletries she could find.

The next few hours were a blur as I sped back and forth along the I-90 to Buffalo International Airport with my mother, who would later return the car home, as I quickly explained the details of my situation. Every aspect of information divulged led to more questions, but it was exciting, as I had never been to New York City. I had only heard intimidating things of the large metropolis that attracts millions of visitors a year to its bright lights!

Only an hour before boarding, I sped up to the Jet-Blue kiosk, my tires screeching against the pavement and just missing the curb. I got out of the driver door, barely missing the oncoming traffic, and raced to the trunk. I hauled out the overflowing suitcase that must have weighed forty pounds, quickly gave my mother a hug and kiss, and headed inside towards the JetBlue terminal to drop off my luggage.

The line leading up to the front desk wasn't as long as normal, so I was able to move through pretty quickly. Next would be going through the TSA. As I headed toward the checkpoint, I turned back towards the main door and saw my mom standing there as her eyes started to well up with tears.

I gave her a small wave with my left hand, and mouthed, "It's okay." She understood and seemed to start feeling better about the abrupt adventure I was about to embark on. My focus returned back to heading towards the TSA line, with my passport and boarding pass in tow, and in that moment, I could feel a new chapter beginning in my life. I could feel things finally starting to fall into place.

My mind was swirling with what had transpired since the morning hours, as I headed to the New York City gate. The gate had already begun their boarding process, so there was no time to rest and collect my thoughts. I worked my way to the check-in desk, presented my boarding pass, and headed down the long narrow hallway towards the aircraft.

I made it to my seat—B12, which reminded me of the townhouse apartment number I lived in during college with my closest friends Anthony and Chris. This quick yet subtle reminder seemed to calm my nerves, as it brought back great memories.

I slid into my seat that conveniently was next to the aisle, put my hands to my eyes and forehead and took a few long deep breaths. As my body continued to relax a smile took shape, as I thought about how in a short hour I would be in the city that never sleeps for the first time. I never thought I would even visit this massive city, but here I was about to take on a new experience for the next half year. It was exciting! It felt good to put away the past and focus on the short term future; it was awesome. As I closed my eyes to try and rest, only one thought came into my tired mind: I'm off to the Big Apple!

As my plane got closer to and circled around the giant metropolis, I could see the city's major landmarks which included the Empire State and Chrysler building. The Freedom Tower had not been built at that time, so only the two large holes remained where the original Twin Towers once stood. I was not fortunate enough to see them in person, but what a sight they must have been as they towered over the other buildings that encompassed the Financial District.

At this hour, the sun was just starting to go down, and I could see the lights of Times Square starting to display themselves to the world. The city skyline was breathtaking to a young man who came from a much smaller city. I sat in the aisle seat stretching my neck to get as close to the window as possible, leaning over the passengers who sat next to me that would block some of the view. It was my first time looking at such a magnificent city, and I wasn't going to let the moment pass me by.

As the wheels touched down on the JFK tarmac, I could feel the overwhelming excitement flow through my veins. I gathered my things and made it downstairs towards the baggage claim. I couldn't help but notice the fast pace at which people were walking. Everyone was in a hurry, with plans that just couldn't wait.

I carefully took my time grabbing my luggage and making my way outside. There I would wait in the long line of people awaiting the line of taxicabs that must have been twenty deep. When my taxicab pulled up, I tossed my luggage into the trunk, sat in the back seat, and prepared for the wild ride to begin.

My destination was the Club Quarters Hotel that overlooked the Twin Tower landmarks along with the base outline of what would become the Freedom Tower and fountain pools. As the cab took me from JFK airport towards Manhattan, I could see all the different suburbs—excuse me, *boroughs*—where families of all different races would co-exist and call home.

As I got closer to the Brooklyn Bridge, it was amazing to see in person and actually drive over something I had only seen in movies. Once on the bridge, the city skyline of Manhattan opened up to fill my entire view. To the far left was the Statue of Liberty, welcoming with her arm raised as if she was saying hello, passing through the east side of Midtown and Uptown Manhattan, all the way to the right, where the Upper East Side and Harlem resided. It was magnificent.

I couldn't believe that this island could fit the millions of people that lived and traveled here on a daily basis. I could feel myself coming alive, feeling the excitement. I had just landed for the first time, but I didn't want to leave. The skyscrapers and the lights were intoxicating, each one taller than the next. I couldn't stop taking pictures of the different landmarks as I was rolling around in the backseat.

When we pulled up to the hotel, I got my luggage and I just stood there for a few minutes, taking it all in. I was here. As I checked into my room that had a nice balcony overlooking the Financial District, I knew I was there for a reason. I took in the skyline; the sun would soon set and the moon would take its place. It was beautiful. I must have sat out on the balcony for hours, just familiarizing myself with my new surroundings, my new playground. What a change from my younger years on Oakridge Drive and Busti Avenue.

In the morning I would start my first day of work at 111 Wall Street and meet my colleagues for the first time. I could barely get any sleep that night. I couldn't wait to walk down Wall Street and see the New York Stock Exchange, Trinity Church, and the other major banks like Deutsche Bank that resided there which made the area the financial capital of the world.

The next morning, as I headed down towards the Citi office, I was quickly swept up in the surging financial working crowd, briskly walking to their respective institutions. I felt I was one of them, even though I would only be there for six months. I got to feel what it was like to walk with the morning crowd, with the big shots and titans of the financial industry. They were all decked out in their fancy blue and grey suits, their shoes freshly shined. I noticed the air about them. They were all so confident, so refined, so in charge. There was nothing they couldn't do.

As I walked to the end of Wall Street, just before I stepped into the office, I looked back up at the historic stone street I had just walked down, looking at Trinity Church peering through the narrow space at the very top. I felt like I belonged. I felt empowered, yet comfortable like I had been doing it for years. It was an unreal feeling. As I stood in the elevator approaching the 21st floor, I could feel the excitement and nervousness building.

The elevator doors gave way to what could have been 100 people walking in and out of aisles, who were on the phone calling the trading desk, were screaming about a PnL break, were slamming their office door. My mind was spinning, but I tried to remain calm and fit in. Good luck with that. In my instructions I knew I had to meet my boss, my new colleagues, and the Director in the conference room that was in the far right corner of the large floor. I walked in, smiled to the people in the room and sat down.

I was sweating through my white dress shirt, as I

was constantly adjusting the navy blue sport coat that was keeping the heat in. As everyone introduced themselves to me, I began to feel comfortable and at ease. I noticed while sitting there, the one side of the table were employees that looked angry and pissed off; on the other side of the table, people that looked as bewildered as I. I didn't fully understand why this was happening.

As the director came in, he started pairing up one person from the left side to one angry person on the right side. This would be the person that would be training me. He was an Asian man probably about 10-15 years older than me, shorter, a little overweight, and had the mouth of a truck driver. Every word was "fuck this and fuck that shit!" It was wild. As the meeting would continue, going over what the training would encompass, I quickly realized why the people across from me were upset and angry. These were the New York City employees that were training away their jobs to the Buffalo employees. They were all receiving severance packages, but would not receive them until they had finished training us, so we could migrate the jobs back to Buffalo for cost cutting reasons.

Over the next several months, until the training was complete, there was a lot of hostility between the trainer and me. I understood; he was married with two children and was losing his job, due to no fault of his own. Once a week, he must have lost his mind on me, standing up shouting and swearing. I just tried to remain calm and refocus him back to the task at hand. It wasn't easy, as this training put us both in a difficult situation, but in the end, the team migration was complete. Our group as a whole supported the Risk Treasury Trading desk which was comprised of bonds, treasuries, futures, swaps and other fixed income products. My part of the process was calculating Profit and Loss statements on a daily basis for the financial product referred to as swaps.

Swaps are a financial tool used for speculating (taking a forward looking view at the market to make profits) or a hedging tool (used to mitigate risk in a trader's portfolio). There are two legs on a basic vanilla Interest Rate Swap: one leg you would pay or receive a fixed rate, while on the other leg you would take the opposite position versus a floating rate, known as the London Interbank Offered Rate or commonly known as "LIBOR." You would net the two associated cash flows, of those two legs, and come up with a "market value."

Based on if this number was higher or lower than the previous day, it would tell you if you were making or losing money based on the difference of those rates. It's a lot take in for people not familiar with financially traded markets. This was the product I would focus on to begin my financial career. It was interesting to see the subject matter I had learned about in Business School being applied to the real world. As the weeks flew by, I was getting better in my position and with the responsibilities that I held. I became comfortable picking up the phone and speaking to the traders whose PnL I was calculating.

Traders are an interesting breed. One moment they are in a great mood, the next moment, they are swearing why the PnL we reported was not what they had expected based on their calculations. The ability to communicate with a frantic trader is an art form that is developed over time, being able to calm them down so they understand the message you are trying to convey to them as to why there is a discrepancy. They are in high pressure positions, with trading activity flowing into their blotters waiting for execution. They balance a million things at once, checking the trades before executing them, monitoring the risk in their portfolios, looking for ways to make money in a lightning fast market. It takes a special person that is passionate about the markets and making money to be good in that position. Over time, I was able to form a good relationship with the three traders I supported. They were highly intelligent and extremely fast talkers, but they treated their PnL product support with respect. I enjoyed working for them. It wasn't easy building up the relationship, but after you helped figure out enough breaks and reported the PnL in their portfolio correct enough times, they began to trust you. Such an important relationship needs to be earned and kept in the financial business. You can be on top of your game for months, but one major slip up and you are starting all over again. It's about consistency. I loved the high pace, the energy. The hours went fast, but there were some very long days, resulting in exhaustion by week's end.

The night life after work was amazing. Between the bars and steakhouses we would visit, my newfound friends and I would eat and drink the night away. It was nothing like I had at home. We would be out until 2 AM in the morning, crash in bed, then be up by 6:30 AM to start the day. It would catch up to you after enough days, but none of us cared; this was a once in a lifetime opportunity. We had to make the most of it. We took cabs to and from work since we had daily food and travel stipends. We mastered the art of free continental breakfasts at the hotel, the street food lunches, then splurged for the big porterhouse steaks and bourbon drinks at night. It was always a great time spending time with co-workers discussing the day's events and the trainer they were working with. I only wished the time would have slowed down.

Time in New York City flies by. I swear the clock moves faster within the confines of the 5 boroughs, then in the rest of the world. The city is truly in its own bubble. The news would flood in about market activity and major events that happened within the city limits. The rest of the world didn't matter because we were in the center of it.

To this day, I can still recall and laugh about when "The Decision" was made by Lebron James in the summer of 2010. The news that he would leave Cleveland and possibly play for the Knicks had the city in a buzz as it was smeared across newspapers and skyscrapers in Times Square that conveyed the day's highlights. People at work couldn't stop talking about it as they had Lebron pasted across their desktop wallpapers.

The New Yorkers were convinced he was playing for their beloved team, as they repeatedly stated there was no point to watch as it was a foregone conclusion. People were trying to find on the internet ways to buy Lebron James Knicks jerseys to celebrate the team's newest addition. That night when it was decided he would leave for Miami instead, the environment the next morning was hostile to say the least, as people would scream about what had transpired that night. "Fuck him, I never liked him, I hope he gets sunburn in Miami!" were the popular quotes that day. I thought it was hilarious; one minute they loved him, the next they wanted to crucify him. Ah, the sports life in New York.

I was grateful to have that experience. On the weekends, a small group that consisted of my close friends Tom and Ron, would go to the water that faced New Jersey, and eat expensive brunches that included salmon, poached eggs, and Bloody Marys. Then we would sit overlooking the water smoking cigars. We were kings. We were saving money, living for free, and experiencing a city life we could only dream of. After a while, as the six months grew to an end, I truly forgot about going back. I had forgotten that this was short-term. I had forgotten that I would have to go back home. I didn't want to, I couldn't get enough of that life; I never wanted it to end.

This was one of the best experiences of my life. I felt that after all the bad things that had happened, I was finally in a good place mentally to continue the climb. I could visualize how my life would be if I lived in an area like this. The friends I would make; the family I would create. I couldn't stop thinking about it. As I packed up my things and headed to the airport, all I could think about was doing whatever it took to get back. To return, but not as a short term stay, but to reside and create a life I had dreamed of. The city tested me mentally, physically, emotionally like no other. It was intriguing, but I had only tasted a small portion, I wanted more. I couldn't wait to come back.

Chapter 6:
Making Big Changes

"In life, you will either find a way to make your dreams come true or you will make excuses. Either way, your results will show which choice you made."

–John Assaraf

I came back to Buffalo from my six-month unforgettable experience in New York City with so much confidence and motivation to carry my life to the next level. I was putting in the longer hours, but it was okay, it was worth it. I couldn't wait to keep pushing forward.

One of my closest friends at Citi when I was working at the Buffalo location during this time was Syudar Rahman. He was in another product control group and sat right behind my desk. The lengthy and skinny guy from Bangladesh had a very nonchalant demeanor, but as I got to know him, I quickly saw the burning desire within him to want better for himself and his family.

His family was located in Uptown Manhattan, around 130th street, but since he went to school at the University of Buffalo, he was hours away from the family he was inspired by and used as the focus of his determination. His father left his family when he was little, launching him into a roll of being the "man of the house." He had a responsibility back home to help out his mother and brother.

His goal was to be a trader within the bank, a tall task for a product controller not coming from a prestigious college and positioned outside the Greenwich office in New York City. That did not stop him though, as he would spend the next five years relentlessly working and fighting for that dream to become a reality.

I have never seen someone more driven and inspiring than "Sy." He knew the odds were small, but it never stopped him. He would get on the morning train at 5:45 AM to arrive at work at 7 AM, work until 8 or even 9 o'clock at night, then take the hour train back home. This would occur day in and day out, but he was relentlessly determined to pursue his dream. He had interviewed several times on different desks, but was promptly rejected for whatever reason they gave each time. He never gave up, he never stopped trying.

The one night when we were out having a beer, I

could see the process was weighing on him and his hope was starting to fade. I told him that he was so close and couldn't give up as he had a promise, a responsibility, to himself and his family to see it through. He would later tell me several months later that those words inspired him to continue his push.

I'll never forget the day I got the text from him stating, "I got it! I'm a trader!" As I read the text, my eyes began to well up with tears. I was so happy for him, more than he would ever know or that I could explain to him. I knew how hard it was for him, putting in those long hours and spending almost three hours a day on a train with one goal on his mind. He is the definition of persistence, determination, and perseverance. I am extremely proud of my friend. How could I ever give up after seeing what he's been through and what he's accomplished? I told him as we met up, how happy and proud of him I was. We both weren't happy in our Product Control roles in Buffalo and wanted more. We were strong enough to demand more for ourselves and realized a better life we had dreamed and talked about so many times before. Sy, you are an inspiration to me in my journey, your story motivated me to keep pushing, and I am grateful to have you as a friend.

After two years at my position, it became too repetitive. I wasn't learning anything new, and I was losing the passion, drive, and momentum that I obtained while away. After Sy left and relocated back to his home in New York City, pursuing his dream to be a trader, all I could keep thinking about was the environment I had come from and the driven people that I had encountered. I needed to get back there, but this time for good. I needed to get back to that environment as it fueled me to be better, to become more, to give and receive more. I had only a small taste, but I needed to return.

As the weeks and months passed, I could feel my old self starting to creep in again. I was starting to become depressed, starting to feel helpless, starting to feel that my life at this point and thirty years in the future would be the same. I kept thinking about the chances I was given, again and again, but what was I doing with them? The relentless thoughts of finding what my purpose was and why I was spared continued to eat at my subconscious. I was starving for change.

When I began to feel this weight on me, this continued pressure I had put on myself, I started to lash out at the ones I loved. Parents, sister, close friends. It didn't matter who it was, as I simply saw them as the reason why I wasn't where I wanted to be, wasn't proud of who I had become. It was their fault, not mine. They were keeping me from my dreams. How dare they? I would have countless arguments and shouting matches with my parents when I would stop home for a visit because my patience and frustration was boiling over. It wasn't right for them to endure this, but I didn't know how else to handle the situation.

After a month or so of this constant arguing, I finally started to take action towards relocating back to New York City. I spoke to the traders that I supported, who agreed to help and put in a good word for me when the time came, which was greatly appreciated, but I needed to get in touch with the manager, whose name was Marcus. I needed to find a way to get his attention so he would consider me for a Middle Office role.

When I reached out to one of the Middle Office support reps, and explained in detail my situation and desire to get back to New York, he agreed to help me get in front of Marcus and hopefully set up an interview. After a few days and consistent follow up, the Middle Office rep helped me set up a phone interview with the manager to discuss my current position, the Middle Office role, and desire to learn more under his guidance in the New York office.

There is a big difference in pace, concentration, and responsibility between Product Control and Middle

Office. Product Control is responsible for the accurate daily PnL calculation and presentation of the Trading desk's performance on a prior day, or T+1, basis. The Middle Office is responsible for the current day's high volume trading activity, which consists of making sure all executed trades flow into the system for risk evaluation and proper, up-to-date reporting within the trading desks portfolio. Middle Office was more stressful and moved at a much faster pace, since it was handling the high volume of the Swap's Desk intraday trading activity.

It is important to note that during this time, many positions were moving from New York City to Buffalo for cost cutting reasons, so it was difficult going against the grain, like a salmon swimming upstream. It was a difficult request, but I kept pushing so the right people, including directors, traders, and human resource employees, heard me.

After the phone interview concluded, the last remaining words by the manager were the dreaded, "Thank you for your time, we will be in touch if we want to move forward." I hated hearing those words as they are almost always a certain "No." I was uneasy for the next few days going over every one of my answers and his responses. I would replay the words I heard, the tone in which those words were expressed, and overanalyze everything.

Finally, all the waiting came to an end when I heard from HR that the manager was impressed with me and wanted to move forward setting up a transfer date for when I would leave Buffalo for New York City. I felt so relieved that Marcus wanted to move forward, I could feel the stress lifted from my shoulders. I could not wait to drive home and tell my parents the great news. My wish had been granted!

Now that I had confirmation from HR that we would work towards a start date, a lot of the pressure had dissipated. I was able to focus on my family again, for a short time anyway, and enjoy two of the most influential events in my life, events that would help change my perspective forever. These special events were the births of my two adorable nephews Nathan and Christopher.

Holding them for the first time was the ultimate joy that would help sustain me for the push to New York City. I remember sitting in the hospital for 10 hours with my parents as we waited for my sister to deliver the newest member to our family, Nathan.

I will always remember my Dad running into one of his closest friends Al in the hospital. He was visiting his daughter who had just given birth that week as well. His words resonated with me when he said to my Dad, "Your life is never going to be the same, only good stuff from here on out Pat" as he smiled and entered the elevator heading down to the lobby.

He was so right as our family's lives would start to mend. Our family had endured many trying times and we were due for a better and uplifting moment. As my sister was getting into the ninth and final tenth hour of labor, my mom had left my dad and me to help my sister with the final steps of the delivery process. It was agonizing for us, not knowing what was going on and if everything was alright. We felt helpless. We would text my mom every 20 minutes until we received an update, then they stopped coming in.

We had no idea what was going on. Was there trouble? Was there something we could help with? We just looked at each other, while trying to stay positive about the unfolding events. We hadn't heard anything for what seemed like eternity, when finally, the text message that changed our lives displayed on my phone: "We're all done, healthy baby, make your way in."

We couldn't speed walk fast enough, as we jostled for positioning to who would leave the waiting room first. As we made our way through the first set of beige colored doors, we saw my mom, as she directed us towards my sister's room. It felt like eternity walking down the long hallway, as I could feel my heart pounding with every step.

When my body crossed the door's threshold, the first person I saw was my sister, who looked exhausted but happy. Then immediately my attention went to the plastic container that held my new best friend. Walking in, we had no idea the sex of the baby.

My sister declared, "Say hello to the baby."

My dad and I looked at each other, at the baby, then back at my sister as we shouted, "What is it?" Then she finally put us out our misery by stating it was a healthy baby boy.

His name was Nathan Patrick. The pressure and anxiety of the moment quickly evaporated. I ran to embrace my sister to congratulate her and her husband. "I'm so happy for you, I'm so happy for you," I yelled into her ear trying to control myself.

Then I went back to the plastic bin where Nathan was lying. The moment his squinty little eyes opened and locked onto mine, I was hooked. Everything changed in that moment, all the problems that were beating me down had dissipated. None of that mattered, there were bigger things for me, bigger responsibilities in my life. I was an uncle!

I couldn't stop looking at him or stay away from where he had been laid comfortably. Eventually we would go home, but not before I got to hold him. As my sister placed him gently into my arms, I felt more love for another person than for myself.

I grew exponentially in that moment. I could feel his warm little body laying across my forearms. I could feel the soft heartbeat as he began to coo as I held him. I was the happiest I had been in a few years, as his hands wrapped around my thumb, and quickly taking another peek at me. He felt like holding a warm loaf of bread. I knew finally what it felt like to love someone unconditionally.

He doesn't know it now, but one day I'll explain to him when he's old enough how he saved my life. How he gave my life a higher purpose, a higher meaning. He changed and influenced my life without saying a word. All it took was a look, a subtle look, and I was at peace.

That feeling only deepened a couple years later when I held his brother Christopher for the first time. I was already in New York City when Christopher was born, but I was fortunate enough to hold him two weeks later. It was agonizing not being there when he was first born, but I accepted the fact that being away would have consequences like missing some birthdays and holidays as the years would pass.

There is nothing better than knowing the influence

you will have on their lives and they don't even know who you are yet, but they will, they surely will. Holding them when they're little is so important as a bond develops and strengthens. It is something I will remember forever. I tried to enjoy the moments as much as possible because you know soon enough they will be too big or such a "big boy" where they won't want to be held. You have to cherish those moments because they go by so fast.

I am proud to be from Buffalo. I will never be afraid to admit that. It takes a certain level of mental toughness to say that you are from Buffalo. When you go to another city you know you will hear a comment about Super Bowls, Stanley Cups, or about the amount of snow we get. You have to brush these comments off or they will affect you.

It's unfortunate those great teams weren't able to win the ultimate prize, but in actuality, I don't feel that our city should be classified just by our sports teams. There is so much more to the area. The area has some of the best dining, culture, architecture, and quality of life in the United States. This comes from a person who has been to New York City, Boston, Philadelphia, Washington, San Diego, Miami, and Tampa Bay among others. These cities don't have any advantage on Buffalo in these areas. Buffalo has this image that there is nothing but bad weather and frankly, stupid and lazy people.

The truth is, I've visited all the above mentioned cities, and I've been caught in snow storms that cause several hour flight delays, hurricanes, tropical thunderstorms, and non-stop rain that would ruin several days of a vacation. No one seems to mention those things about the other cities, and let's not forget stupidity and laziness is apparent everywhere. I haven't seen a city that has better quality and higher character of people, who will go the extra mile for a family member, neighbor, or complete stranger, than the ones in Buffalo. Many of the people I know are very intelligent, hardworking, and driven people that would thrive in any city on this planet.

Since I have moved to New York City, when I hear someone make a comment in my presence, I stand up for my hometown. After they make their comment, I always ask, "So I assume that you have visited Buffalo?" The shocking thing is, 95% of the people I ask that to have never been to the city. The ignorance astounds me that people in their late 20's and 30's, who have obtained degrees from prestigious colleges, wouldn't explore the subject matter before opening their mouths.

I left Buffalo because I wanted to take my life to the next level, where there was endless opportunity in

the field of finance, and see if I could feed off the energy
that New York City has and see where it would take me.
I left Buffalo because I needed a change and at that time,
as I wasn't mentally strong enough to succeed there. I
needed to become more knowledgeable in my craft, and
be around other people who would drive and push me to
be better.

Back home, I was too comfortable and it led to
making horrible and stupid decisions that I have paid
for over and over again. I let people talk me out of my
dreams and goals, and I take full responsibility for that
now, but I didn't back then. I needed to have thicker
skin, I needed to be more. I was starting to drown again,
and I couldn't go back to the way things used to be.

I needed the people who have cared for me for so
long to feel like the time and money they invested was a
good decision. I had been taking money from the people
I loved and I was wasting it. No more. It needed to stop,
it needed to end. I needed to leave and start my own life.
I needed to see if I could put be dropped into a "jungle"
and survive without help. I needed to see what I was
made of. That's why I left Buffalo, and not because it's a
bad place, but because I needed a chance to change with
a fresh start. Period.

When the time is right, and I have sustained the

right mental attitude and I've achieved what I want to in New York City, I will return and continue to build the resurgence of the Buffalo area. I will put my stamp on the city that runs through my veins, pulsates through my mind on a constant basis, and makes my heart beat faster when I know I am near. Every time I visit, the exact moment the airplane tires hit the floor mat of the runway, and impact is made, I know I am home. I no longer have any worries. When I arrive, and my father drives me from the airport towards Hamburg I remember my childhood, I remember the familiar landmarks that have shaped me as I pass downtown Buffalo, I remember the faces of my family members who are alive and who are no longer with me on this earth. Most importantly, I remember my home. This is the promise I have made to myself, for which I have a responsibility, and to the great place that I am from.

CHAPTER 7
THE CORE GROUP

"If my mind can conceive it, and my heart can believe it,
then I can achieve it."
—Muhammad Ali

As it became clearer that I would be uprooting myself back to the city that had breathed new life into my once listless lungs, it was tough stepping away from the family and friends that I had grown up with for most of my life. I knew I wouldn't see or speak with them as much anymore, and as time would pass, they would begin to drift away. It was sad to think about this, but I knew I would remain close with my core group of friends. These were the people that were by my side for many years, the ones that I could depend on. The ones that knew me the best.

In life, if you are fortunate enough, you will have that one person or small group of friends that you can rely on, depend on, confide in, and be vulnerable around. Not everyone will get the key to your innermost thoughts, dreams, and fears, so you must be careful who you give it out to. It can be scary if you have been neglected or taken advantage of in the past, but I believe feeling uncomfortable and allowing the right people in are key to success.

A person can go through their whole life and not find that person, but if you are fortunate enough, when you have them, you know it. They are meant to build you up, and you in turn will do the same for them. They are there for the entire journey; they see your development, through all of your triumphs and all of your failures. They are not there to judge, but instead, provide guidance along the way. They are there for it all, they are the constant. It's not about jealousy or having a hidden agenda, it's about being there for them and having receiving the same in return. They are there to lift you up and keep you in check when needed, to make sure you are in line with your short term and long term goals. In short, they are the bedrock of your being.

I was fortunate enough to have a small group that emerged at different points of my life. These close people for me were Brandon, Anthony, and Tom. Brandon and Anthony were friends from my neighborhood. These friends I went to elementary school with, while Tom I met during my time in Citi, first meeting him when I touched down in New York City. It was a great group because they all had qualities I could admire.

Brandon was extremely competitive like me; we would push each other in sports, school, and in careers. We had a good balance of healthy competition, but it was balanced by the respect we had for each other.

Anthony was more the strong, silent type. He didn't waste his words, was very direct, and could be trusted to keep sacred conversations shared amongst us that no one else was entitled to. If you told Anthony something you wanted private, you could rest assured that he would keep it close to the vest. He had the integrity and had built a reputation over many years of keeping his word and delivering when he made a promise. He was never caught gossiping like so many others. He had qualities that few obtain and keep in this world.

Tom was very confident, almost to the level of arrogance, but his work ethic was matched by few I've seen. He sometimes carried the persona like he didn't care, but he was one of the most thoughtful friends I've had the pleasure of encountering. Being away in New York City, Tom would still stay in touch, regularly asking how things were and how I was doing. He would give me financial advice when needed to further build my retirement IRA and company 401(K) funds. He had the focus and discipline that few show, while obtaining a deeper know-edge base in the area of finance, validated when he recently achieved the Chartered Financial Analyst Certification for his years of razor sharp focus.

They all had such great qualities I could admire, and together, they formed a certain level of perfection one would need in a great friend.

I met Brandon first on the neighborhood streets of Oakridge Drive and would become the closest with him over the twenty year friendship we shared. I still remember the first time we met. I was standing on the end of my driveway, in the middle of summer after my family had just finished moving in, and was looking for a friend as I was new to the neighborhood. I remember Brandon was in his driveway shooting the basketball towards his NBA style glass backboard. I thought the backboard was so cool.

He was by himself, but seemed like a nice person. We were in the 4th grade at the time, but he was considerably taller than me or others in that age group. He had to be very close to six foot, with jet-black hair, and braces. He liked to wear a lot of sports shirts either of the Buffalo Bills or Adidas apparel. His voice would crack at times, but it was ok, since he seemed like an honest and kind person.

We would develop a close friendship as we shared many classes together in elementary, middle and high school. He was quiet around other people in school, but once we got home, the muzzle was removed, and he would share all of his thoughts and feelings with me. Over time, I would share my thoughts and innermost feelings with him as well. The bond was strong between us; we were like brothers. We would frequently visit each other's home and became close with the other's parents.

We would spend numerous weekends playing football, basketball, and hockey. We always were on separate teams which fueled a healthy level of competition between us. We would not hold back on each other, finishing checks or tackles when we would play hockey and football respectively.

We would play with other friends in the neighborhood, which is how I met Anthony, for hours on end until we would be completely exhausted. As we entered high school we focused on our respective sports, football for him, and hockey for me, but we always supported each other at games in the season and practiced drills in the summer in the offseason to help the other achieve the next level as we climbed from Freshman level to Varsity. We would travel to Six Flags or the local Erie County Fair in the summers.

As we got older, we would travel to Mexico with his brother Dan, and Tom. It was one of the best trips of my life and I was glad we were able to share the experience with each other. I still remember on that vacation, the one night Brandon and I left the others behind at the resort and traveled the hour to Cancun for the night in a hotel rental car. It was amazing traveling by ourselves and heading inside the stadium-sized club called the Bulldog. There had to be ten thousand people—if not more—with a dance floor on the ground level, a full bar at either end, with thousands more on the upper deck. It was nothing we had ever seen before. We partied into the early morning hours then headed back to the resort while smoking cigars. It was an incredible night meeting and dancing with people from other cultures. It was an amazing experience because we shared it together.

A few months later, it was difficult when he announced he was moved to Virginia on a government work assignment. I was happy for him, but it felt lonely at times because he wasn't around to share feelings and special events with. The time helped us grow as individuals, without having the other as a crutch. We would begin to develop our own personalities and lives for the first time without one another. It was difficult at first, but it was a good lesson that taught me to be strong in my own skin and be able to rely on myself. He was someone I could rely on, someone I could trust, but as time passed, we began to grow apart. I believe we had become products of our environment, as he worked closely with ex-Marines, and I with financial traders and brokers. They were just two totally different surroundings that didn't mesh well together.

He would be away from home for seven years before I made my move to New York City. I still recall the countless phone calls we would have between one another discussing how things were different and how we would see less of each other as time progressed. We would still visit one another a couple times a year, but it wasn't the same. It wasn't like the good old days. He always had a vision of us finding that special woman in our lives, raising our separate families, and living as neighbors in Virginia. The problem was that I didn't share the same vision. My life wasn't going to be in Virginia, as New York City was my focus and long term stay.

Once I received my official letter at Citi and my leaving date for New York City approached, Brandon had come home to visit his family, but to also wish me well on my journey. We wanted to celebrate at a local bar located about 2 miles from my parents' house, who I was staying with before I would leave for the foreseeable future.

It was just the two of us, like it had been for so many times, where we shared so many great memories. On this night though, it was different—it just felt different. The night started off like so many others: seeing common friends that we shared, relaxing at a table close to the bar, and catching up with what was going on in each other's lives. We had shared thousands of nights like this.

As the night progressed, and celebratory shots were shared for the success and great changes that we had been experiencing, the mood changed. It didn't end with food at a local diner. When we started to feel the effects of the night's events, it was time to head back home.

I didn't drive that night because we both understood the ramifications if I drank and dared to attempt driving home. If I was pulled over and arrested, it would be the second time in less than 3 years. The ramifications would be severe. It would be my second drunk driving offense that would result in a felony charge, placing me in jail, and any hope for the future would be completely lost.

We both knew this. We knew what it would do to my life.

The problem was that he didn't want to leave his car at the bar. We knew that he would have to drive, and he had been understanding up to this point. This time was different. As we were closing up our respective bar tabs, he kept mentioning how he didn't want to leave his car and he didn't want to have one of our parents pick us up.

"How about a cab?" I suggested.

"No, not too many come around this area, at this time of the night," he replied. He was right as it was about 3 AM, and in a small suburb 20 minutes from the city, not too many taxi cabs would be in the area. He kept pushing for me to drive, as he kept saying "Come on, I can't leave my car here."

Over and over he said this, until I had had enough. Once we were outside, I couldn't hold it in anymore, as I shouted "Do you know what this would do to me?"

This lack of judgement would result in no New York City, no life, no anything. I continued to shout as I could feel my heartbeat pulsating through my head and in my arms as they shook with nervousness and fear of what was being requested of me. There had been this growing tension as the end of the night neared, I could sense it in the tone of his voice, and I could see it in his eyes.

I needed to ask. "Do you even give a shit if I was pulled over and arrested?" I don't know if it was the alcohol taking over us at that moment, but I was shocked by his response. I expected him to say that of course he knew, that he was sorry for continuing to push, that he knew how severe the situation was and that we would find another way home.

Instead, all I received was a blank stare. No words, no emotion, no facial expression, nothing, just silence. It felt like eternity before he said, "I don't know man." That was it, nothing more was said between us on the two mile walk back home, as his car remained in the parking lot. What a long distance to travel when the friendship you thought you had, for so many years, which was so strong, was in fact paper thin.

Maybe it wasn't ever that strong to begin with, but I'd like to think it was. In those moments, as we took one step at a time towards home, passing by familiar places where we used to play as children, one hardening truth was clearly evident from that night: our friendship had changed. We had grown apart. It was sad, it was disappointing, but it was the painful reality.

We would continue to talk for the next few months, visiting each other in our respective cities, but it wasn't the same. We would argue and curse at each other. During this time all I could think was, "What were we doing? This wasn't the friend I knew, the one I could trust with my closest secrets. The one I knew since the fourth grade. Had we really become enemies?"

Eventually we mutually decided to move on. We would place blame on other things, outside factors like our significant others, but it was because neither of us wanted to focus on the harsh reality that our friendship had disintegrated for some time. It wasn't salvageable anymore.

I know it wasn't easy for either one of us, but I'd like to believe that we are better off today, and happier because of what resulted that night. We needed to know where we stood with each other. We needed to have mutual respect for each other. We needed to be better friends towards one another. I don't think either of us liked what the other person had become, but it was clear that there wasn't mutual respect anymore. Respect is the foundation of any friendship, any relationship. When it's not there anymore, it's time to move on. Sadly, our friendship was done.

CHAPTER 8:
ON TO NEW YORK CITY

"Everything you want is on the other side of fear."
—Jack Canfield

After an unusually long transfer process—one that normally takes a month or two at most had dragged on for over six months and included weekly follow ups—the day had finally arrived. There were times that I believed it would fall through, but I never gave up hope. I had a vision in my mind and trusted my gut that it would materialize.

My transfer had been approved and I was simply waiting for my start date to be provided by my new boss. The move really hit home, as I was starting to plan on what would be taken and what would be left behind. It was an exciting time. I had focused on this moment ever since my feet last stepped off the sidewalks of Midtown Manhattan and had returned to Buffalo. I needed to keep the momentum going from my last visit, and realize my dream, but I understood that this time would be different. I wouldn't be a visitor anymore; I would become a mainstay.

My life's trajectory would rise, based on the endless opportunities and potential that the city would offer—not only for my career, but from a social aspect as well. I needed this change in the worst way, as I could feel my stay at home had been too long. My mental edge was starting to fade away. I needed it to return before it would be too late, and I would slide back into my old self. That wasn't an option this time, as I had run out of chances.

Once the start date of June first was confirmed, the move was set. I had one week to get my things packed, transported to the city, and set up. This would be just in time for my first day of work. There was only one slight problem: I had nowhere to live.

My father and I quickly combined our airline miles to cover the cost of the flight and made our way down to the city. Our home base for the trip would be at the Club Quarters in Midtown. Since I never needed to take the subway in my last extended visit, and had never taken it before, I needed to be close to a major landmark. This location would need to be my central hub. I knew a lot of trains went through Manhattan, but I needed to narrow my search.

Bingo! Madison Square Garden came to mind. Was it close to a major subway lines and a central point? You better believe it. It sits directly on top of Penn Station. From that point, I could connect to any train line coming in or going out of the city. This area, 34th street and 8th avenue, would be my focus.

When we touched down, there was no time to reminisce about the great memories I experienced before; it was time to get to work. Operation "find an apartment" was in full effect, and ranked with the highest level of severity. I was able to find a broker through a mutual friend whose brother was living in the area. I quickly gave him a call the day before so he could put together a list of apartments for us to see. He knew the time frame was tight, as I was only there for three days, and needed to see a high number of apartments to give myself as many options as possible.

When we met up to start our journey through Midtown, all I could remember was how hot it was. It was the dead of summer, in late June, with temperatures in the high eighties. If you were on a beach with a nice breeze during that time, it would be perfect. In this situation, we would be walking up and down stairs, up and down streets and avenues, and in and out of the subway. This was going to be rough.

The first thing we purchased after we made it to the city was large Poland spring water bottles to assist us during the operation. We took the 7 AM flight and were in the city by almost 9 AM. The search had begun.

All the buildings bled together, and everything looked very nice from the online pictures, but this isn't the reality of New York City living for most. What you saw on the pictures wasn't necessarily what you would get when you looked inside. In addition, if you found a place you liked, you better be willing to shell out the month's rent, broker fee and deposit to secure your top choice. There is so much competition that if you see a place that you like and walk out of the building, there's a good chance you are kissing that apartment goodbye. The total initial fee that included first months rent, broker fee and upfront deposit, would be anywhere from $6,000 to $10,000 for a nice place.

The first place we saw, I will never forget. It was a studio apartment, as I would be living by myself and needed to cut costs as much as possible. It was on the cheaper side—$1,000 per month—so why not check it out?

We opened the door and the total apartment couldn't have been more than 200 square feet. There was space for a small closet, a single bed, a stove that was

142

right next to the bed, and a small bathroom and shower. There was only enough room to fall into the bed, stand up, and go to the bathroom.

I was blown away, as I had never seen a New York City apartment before. I had no idea that people could live this way and keep their sanity. Even prison inmates have more room. After quickly dismissing this idea, we needed to up the price of our search to $2,000 per month, as I would need much more space. This was an eye opening experience.

We would continue to see nine other apartments during that day. After seeing a few apartments, everything was a blur and unfortunately, I had found nothing close to something I would be able to comfortably call home. I found narrow apartments as wide as a hallway, larger kitchen apartments that included just enough room for a bed, or ones that were below ground level with no natural light.

It's incredible when you would search one by one and notice things that you cannot live without. The bare necessities were sometimes too much to ask. It was okay, because we still had two more days to search. Heading back to the hotel, my dad and I were tired, but still in good spirits.

After a long day, we went for a quiet dinner at a local pub, which included cheeseburgers and tall Sam Adams beers, to cap off an eventful first day. We discussed what we had seen during the day, and planned out what were our "must haves" for day two. The list of must haves included: some natural light, location needed to be close to the A, C, E subway lines that would take me to work down on Canal Street in lower Manhattan, rent no more than $2,000 (or a little more if it included electricity or gas) and most importantly, enough living space to move around in. Maybe even enough space to exercise in, but I would need to temper those expectations after what I had seen after day one.

The next day would include more of the same. Up and down stairs of three floor walkups, where I would leave my dad at ground level unless I found something that was worth his trip. Imagine in and out of building at the foot of the stairs, and my dad saying "Okay, let me know, yes or no" then two-three minutes later me walking back stating "No."

Apartment after apartment, no after no. "How about this one?"

Then I would return with a resounding, "No, no, no!" I was getting more tired and frustrated. By the end of day two, I was beat. My frustration was starting to show; it was starting to boil over. I only had one day left.

I was running out of time. I needed to rest before I lost my mind and said something I would regret to either my dad or the broker. I wouldn't quit—I had put so much effort into this move, I had to find something I liked.

As day three began, we saw more and more of the same old apartments. One had a good size bedroom, but no living space. One had a good living space, but no room for a bed. I didn't know what to do. One after another, and nothing to show for the hard work, the traveling, the countless flights of stairs I had climbed, and the countless steps taken.

The morning went into the afternoon. My dad and I were unraveling as he yelled, "Michael, what are you going to do? There's nothing that we like. Maybe it's just better you just stay home."

I couldn't do this; I had to keep looking, keep searching, because I was meant to be here. I owed it to myself to keep going. My flight out was at 7 PM, and I had to leave the city at 5 PM to catch the flight.

It was 2:30 PM and I had one last chance, one last shot at finding my place. As we stopped to take a breath and get more ice water, the broker looked at me with a worried face as his forehead scrunched and he nervously adjusted his glasses with his hand.

"You may not like this, but it has an elevator and

has good light. You want to check this one out?"

What did I have to lose? "Okay," I said, knowing full well this probably wouldn't work either. We walked to 45th street and approached the Camelot apartments. As I walked in, I was greeted in the lobby by the pleasant doorman as he directed me to the elevator. Heading up to the fifteenth floor, my hopes started to climb with each passing number.

When the elevator stopped and the doors opened, we took only a couple steps to the waiting apartment. When the broker opened the door and I took my first step in, I knew this was the place. The solid brown door revealed a large living room space with plenty of light shining through and hardwood floors that went from the door to the far wall that had four large windows that presented a panoramic view of the midtown skyline. It displayed Times Square and viewed 8th avenue from 45th street down as far as the eye could see.

As I walked around the corner of the apartment, I saw that it had a good size bedroom that would comfortably fit my queen size bed and included two large closets to hold my business and weekend casual attire. Going around the next corner, I found a full bathroom with a good-sized shower. The last room, which was back where the front door resided, was a tucked away kitchen that fit the stove, refrigerator and countertop with light brown wooden cabinets.

As I stepped out of the kitchen and looked at the surprisingly happy faces of my dad and the broker, they knew what my next four words out of my mouth would be. "This is the one!"

With my checkbook and important financial documents in tow, I was ready to put down the deposit and first month's rent. I was prepared for this moment, and there was no way this apartment was going to someone else. This was the place. This would be where I would take the next step towards my "dream scenario." This would be *my* place.

An hour later, the rental agreement was printed out and displayed in front of me to sign. I quickly read through the agreement, signed it, and cut two checks to secure my new residence. Heading down the elevator, I cut the third and final check to the broker for his services.

After viewing several apartments in just under three days, I had found my new place. What a weight that had just been lifted off my shoulders, as I could feel the tenseness in my brow and shoulders immediately dissipate. After arriving back down to ground level, my dad and I shook the broker's hand then quickly returned to the hotel, grabbed our luggage, caught a cab and sped off towards the airport.

We were exhausted but we had completed our mission. There was no stopping us now as we gave each other a quick high five and whispered simultaneously, "Yesss." We closed our eyes, with grins on our faces, after looking back on what we had accomplished. That was a great day for my dad and me. I was glad he was by my side and he put the time in to make sure I found the right place. We did it, and most importantly, we did it together.

Only a few days later we would be back to the tall brick building called Camelot, but this time in a U-Haul with all my worldly possessions. We had spent the 7 hour drive from Buffalo to Midtown Manhattan with little conversation. The trip had moments of laughter but mostly it consisted of small talk, as no one wanted to talk about the obvious fact that I was moving to another city and that life was going to drastically change.

Up and down the elevator went up the boxes, box spring and mattress. One by one. It took us nearly 5 hours to get everything upstairs, unpacked, and set up, and finally, we were done. The move in was an exhausting process but it was complete. As we ate at the Florentine Bistecca, we enjoyed each other's company and just reminisced about the old times. It was good to focus on those memories of family vacations to Florida and Mexico, high school graduations, and my sister's wedding. It was nice to share a nice meal with them before they headed back home the next morning.

In the morning, my parents and I had a quick breakfast, since they wanted to head out of the city and into the Lincoln tunnel before the traffic would increase. After giving them a long hug and kiss, it was time for them to leave. It was sad to see them go as our eyes started to well up with tears. We had been through a lot in the past few years. So many great memories, but so many obstacles that had been overcome.

As they pulled out of the parking lot and started to head down the street, heading further and further away, the reality quickly set in. I could feel the cold sweat taking over my body. It felt like I was a child being dropped off at school for the first time. For a moment I thought, "What am I doing? I'm all by myself! I don't know about this."

As quickly as those feelings came, luckily, they left my subconscious. My confidence quickly came back, as I was ready to start the next chapter in my life. This is what I had been waiting for: an opportunity to build on the fresh start I was given. I had to make the most of it, there was no turning back now. This was it. Let's go.

Feeling comfortable as soon as possible was important, so over the next couple days, I would familiarize myself with my surroundings. Finding where the grocery store, dry cleaners, and favorite spots I would like to enjoy food were located was critical. I would use the Yelp app to tell me what locations were the closest, then make my rounds to the important places that I would need on a weekly basis. This helped me get used to using the local subway and navigate on the street once above ground.

Over the next several months, I would take the subway from the west side to the east side, then up and down on the different lines, traveling to see landmarks like Union Square, Wall St., Empire State Building, and Rockefeller Center. Once I had Manhattan down and I was comfortable I ventured out to Brooklyn, Long Island City, the Bronx and Astoria Queens.

I would pick one landmark in each of the areas, spend the day there, then make my way back to the apartment as the sun would go down. I visited Yankee Stadium in the Bronx, Citi Field in which the New York Mets play in Queens, the "Dumbo" area in Brooklyn, the popular 30th avenue in Astoria, and even Coney Island. Not only was I becoming more familiar with traveling over time, but I was gaining confidence in exploring my new location.

New York City is like no other place in the world. You can have any type of food, night life, drink, or clothing that you desire. From different flavored mojitos at Havana's in Midtown Manhattan to the strongest frozen Margarita's at Two Turtles in Astoria, from the 40/40 club on the East Side to the Gansevoort Rooftop Bar in the Meatpacking District, the city has you covered.

If it exists in the world, it is in New York City. It's the only place I know where you can go to a bar to watch a World Cup soccer match, walk in the first floor all dedicated to the Italian match, surrounded by hundreds of blue jerseys, go up a flight of stairs to see Brazilian fans decked out in a sea of yellow, then go to the top floor to see Germany in a classic "white out" scene.

The entire building was packed with passionate fans who would scream in their native tongue, until their lungs gave out and their voices were hoarse. What made that experience unforgettable was that all three teams won their respective matches, which made for a three floor party that flowed into the streets of Midtown, where people of all different parts of the world gathered over a pint and to root for their team without any arguments or hostility.

Only in the city can you have a Broadway musical like "Kinky Boots" be located right next to a gentleman's club, which was a few steps from a small but delicious cookie shop called Schmackary's. Where else could you be standing in line for their famous cookies, be ridiculed by a teenage group passing by, then two minutes later see them at the end of the line wondering what all the fuss was about? Nowhere else.

The major aspect of the city that intrigued me the most was that people from all different religions, ethnicities, and beliefs can co-exist under one roof or within the confines of one city and be at peace with one another. Every group has their festival or parade that portrays the best parts of their culture. Everyone gets their day to show off their countries colors with pride. It was a major shock at first for a young man struggling to find his way, coming from Buffalo that consisted mainly of white suburban surroundings. It was amazing to me that we could all celebrate the best aspect of each other's background and culture, culminating towards the one aspect that we all enjoy, and that is the food.

Before coming to New York City, the most diverse meal I had ever had was a Mexican burrito. Now, I have tried and loved Thai, Ethiopian, Indian, Brazilian, Chinese, Japanese, Mediterranean, Middle Eastern as specific as Afghanistan, of course Italian, and I know I'm leaving out countless others. You can enjoy a delicious burger at

PJ Clarke's or a massive Porterhouse at Peter Lugers. They all used different spices that excite and invigorate different senses. I couldn't get enough. My goal was and still is, to taste and savor it all while I am here, and then go back for seconds.

I believe that is why people in different parts of America and even around the world gravitate to New York City. You can have any experience you want and, for the most part, enjoy it without any problem. The city will show you the best the world has to offer, from a luxury penthouse suite overlooking Central Park to a five star rooftop bar that provides a panoramic view of the Manhattan Skyline. It can make you believe and truly feel that you can achieve whatever you set your sights on. I also believe people flock to the city to start over or become who they've always wanted to be, when they weren't accepted in their hometown. People can truly be themselves here, for better or for worse, and be happy and at peace.

Living in the city isn't like the movies, however, where everyone lives in an apartment that is the size of a palace or centrally located near a famous landmark. People sacrifice and strive to be successful in the city. It isn't for the faint of heart. It can chew you up and spit you out if you're not careful. It can welcome you with open arms in one moment, and slam the door in your face in the next. Everyone strives and works hard to make it here and that is what gravitated me to the city that never sleeps.

I would start work at my new job at Citi located on Greenwich Street by taking the A line getting off at Canal Street. Coming out of the subway stop and making my way to street level, I immediately noticed the sense of calm and quietness on the lower part of Manhattan. I looked to the right to see the Maserati dealership displaying the beautiful and newly released models for the street traffic. Heading towards the Hudson River that overlooked Hoboken New Jersey, I could see the beautiful high rise lofts and condominiums for the upper class members of the city.

What a beautiful and inspiring place to visit, especially when fall hits and you can see the cast of brown, orange, and yellow leaves on the trees! Towards the water, at the end of the street, was the exquisite thirty-nine floor skyscraper on 388 Greenwich St. The complex with the neighboring ten story grey and red building was where all the trading floors resided, and my new business venture.

I made the transition to New York when a lot of Middle Office and Operational positions were heading back to my hometown. I was grateful for building a relationship with a friend named Vincent that used to support that group, but had moved onto begin his two-year rotation for the Trading and Sales desks. He was off to do great things. He had the motivation, charisma, and confidence to make it happen. He inspired me to want to come to the city and do great things when I arrived. I will always be grateful for his help. He helped me go against the current, and gave me the opportunity to change my life. I hope he achieves all the great things he inspires to be in this life. They simply don't make them like "Vinny."

I was so excited to get started on my first day, as I made my way through security and up the elevator. I could see and feel the energy of the bustling crowd as they made their way to their respective floors, stopping to grab a coffee or a quick chat with a familiar face as they discussed the previous day's market movement. I loved the energy, I loved the pace, and it was what I wanted and what I was hoping for.

I made my way to the third floor and was greeted by my new manager. As he walked me towards the trading floor, I could feel the heat coming off the glass door that encompassed the two-section, forty row behemoth space. As he opened the door, I saw firsthand what it was like to be on an active trading floor at a major bank.

All the Trading and Sales desks, along with Middle Office support, were located up and down the long rows. Each row was split up for the different products that they supported, including Swaps, Risk Treasury, and Foreign Exchange to name just a few.

As I made my way to the left corner and down the rows towards the Swaps Middle Office group, I could see row after row of several Sales and Trading desks that included four monitor computer stations with attached Bloomberg terminals. Everyone was shouting back and forth on the best level for a particular trade being made at that split second. People were on the phone, shouting to their broker or counterpart.

The energy was high, but I thought it was exciting. I was introduced to my colleagues that I would work with directly on the desk, and indirectly with the other groups that supported other financial products like options, futures, and bonds.

As I took my seat, I could not help but notice the staring neighbor to the left of me. He was Asian American, and had quite the flare for the dramatics. He had an explosive and highly energetic personality, but initially seemed like a good person.

As my manager headed down the row to his station, my new friend quickly greeted me with a large smile and the welcoming message: "We're not friends, my goal is to send you back to the hick town in Buffalo that you came from!"

I was blown away. I didn't even know this person or his name yet, and this is how I was treated. I thought to myself, "Is this what it's like on a trading floor?" I would later find out that Lee was not the norm, as the trading floor was full of professionals with high character and integrity. Some of the closest friends I have to this day from the city, I met on that floor.

As the weeks passed, and after several blowups from Lee directed solely at me, early in the morning before the managers were around, I found out why my friend had been so hostile. It was rumored that I was hired to replace my colleague. Once he had heard this information, he made it his goal to make sure that never happened.

As months went on, and the daily ripping would continue, I am impressed to say I kept my cool and pro-fessional attitude. I could understand the fear of losing a job when you have a family to support and little children who depend on you. I get it. What I don't forgive is the actions of a 40-year-old who wasn't happy and didn't even enjoy his job, as he stated on numerous occasions. I wish he had the courage to make changes in his life and go after the things he enjoyed, instead of settling for his current predicament. He was a very smart and knowledgeable person, but there were other ways to handle the insecurities.

I believe you have to enjoy the work that you do; find a purpose and figure out why you get up every morning, get dressed and make your way to work by car or subway train. It's a shame that some people hate their jobs and cannot find peace or internal enjoyment during their day to day lives.

It's important for you to enjoy your work because if you are passionate about the work you perform, you will thrive in that environment setting. If you dread getting up in the morning and struggle through your day, and cannot find happiness or purpose in what you are doing, it's time for a change.

You cannot let an excuse or reason force you to continuously torture yourself. I do believe you need to stick it out over a certain period of time and see if things change, then have the courage to make a change, if in the end if it's not making you happy. Everyone has that internal clock that will eventually go off if their needs and goals are not being met. This will invigorate movement and action that will lead to greater and more fulfilling results.

It is also important to find that balance with work and your outside life. You can thoroughly love and enjoy your job, but if you cannot balance your attention between work and your home life, you will be left having a relationship with your career. Maybe that is fine for some, but I believe the best relationship you can have in this life, the one that will invigorate all your senses and push you to be the best version of yourself, is the one with another person. It's so important to develop the skill of balancing, so that you can benefit from every aspect of your life.

Lastly and most importantly, I also feel strongly that if you dread going to work because of another person you only have two options: you can go on taking the abuse while that person takes your confidence, self-esteem, and self-worth, or you can stand up for yourself and fight back.

As my coworker's abusive behavior continued, after one full year, early in the morning, I had had enough. I sat down to hear the barking begin, but this time I finally unleashed back.

All I remember is saying the words "Fuck You" until he stopped talking. Over and over again, I would repeat myself, until his mouth finally shut. I lost track of how many times I said those words.

He looked back and said, "What's wrong with you?" I just smiled back and began my day. From that moment on, I didn't hear a peep out of Lee. I should have done that a long time ago, but I was glad I finally did.

After a year and a half, I would find out many notes that I had taken under his "guidance" were incorrect, but I would learn plenty more about the swap product from the other colleague in my group named Bill.

Bill is another high-class individual, who is an outstanding person, and I wish him nothing but the best. At the end of the day, when people would leave, he would go through the system with me step by step to understand the product at a deeper level and how all the different pieces of my job fit together. He had just gotten married, and I'm sure would have enjoyed more time with his wife, but he stayed. He could see my confidence was fading over that time, but I applaud him for assisting someone who was in need.

I still read and implement the notes taken under him today. After the last note was taken, when credibility and trust in my work was recognized by the traders that I directly supported, I felt it was time to move on. I had been in the Banking Industry most of my career, and after five years, I wanted to see what other opportunities were available in the city. I learned a lot about myself, the financial culture, and how to fight through and stay calm in a high paced and stressful environment. I wouldn't have traded that experience for everything. I left that trading floor with much more confidence and determination than when I first entered.

CHAPTER 9:
FINDING "THE ONE"

"Opportunities don't happen. You create them."
—Chris Grosser

The past year and a half had made me grow up. It made me become more mature and learn to trust and rely on myself—more than I had ever done before. It made me fully aware of how tough and demanding living in New York City could be. It is not for the faint of heart. It takes a special type of person to be successful there. Don't be mistaken: I could not have made this climb without my parents, Mary and Patrick, and my sister Michele. I am indebted to them for the rest of my life for the love and support they provided through the dark times.

They are not alone though. My special and beautiful girlfriend Liliana had a big part in this process as well, as she stood by me since we first met shortly after I moved to New York City and helped me endure my first year and a half at Citi in a new location. One week after I moved into my apartment, I was invited to my close friend Brandon's engagement party. I had no idea that that evening would change my life forever.

As I take myself back to that engagement party, making my way to Virginia for the party, I felt a sense of calm and reassurance as I rode the Vamoose bus from Manhattan to Arlington. I felt at peace for the first time in a while. With so many new things happening so quickly in my life, it was a nice change of pace to slow things down and take a step back. I was so happy for my friend. I had known Brandon for so long and was happy to see him take the next step in his life.

I could see he was happy as we got closer to the event. He and his wife were nervous, understandably so, as we all got ready for the dinner and special moment we would all share together.

As we drove in his car, heading for his fiancé's home where the event was held, I'll always remember when we parked and I took my first step out of the car. As I stepped out, I was hit intensely by the bright rays of the sun. My entire view was encompassed by the yellow, red, and white rays.

Having blue eyes, this is especially painful, as my eye color is extremely sensitive to the light. This is always something I try to stay away from, since I can feel the rays painfully piercing through my irises.

In this moment, however, I was unusually comfortable. I had this sense of calm about me as I headed inside. It was a wonderful feeling and something I hadn't felt before. As the evening went on I would meet mutual friends, reconnect with my friend's parents and siblings, and introduce myself to the bride's family and friends. The evening was a lot of fun as I was sharing an important moment with one of my best friends.

After appetizers and drinks were consumed, it was time for the thank you speeches by the engaged couple. As my friend started to speak, I felt a pressure on my focus to turn to the left and examine the group of people who were there to enjoy the event. Scanning across every person my attention was immediately grabbed by a beautiful and sophisticated woman.

I couldn't stop focusing on the profile of her pretty face and the curves of her body. I was immediately drawn in, as I could hear her laugh at a comment made by the bride. I needed to meet this special lady. I didn't know how to introduce myself, but that didn't matter. What mattered was that I made it my goal, by the end of the night, to learn more about this intriguing woman.

I admit, I needed some liquid courage before

approaching the group she was in, but desperate times called for desperate measures. I knew she had headed outside to the porch with a few friends, none of which I knew at the time, but I was determined to make my way in.

I flung the door open, taking my first few steps onto the porch, and declared, "So this is where all the young people are?" I saw a chair conveniently open next to her and with no hesitation, I proceeded to sit down. "Hi, I'm Mike, what is your name?" I know I could have drawn up a better opening line, but I needed to know her name, so I was direct and straight to the point.

She calmly replied, "Liliana, are you a friend of the groom?"

What a pretty name! I wanted to know more. "Yes I am, are you from the area?" I asked.

"Yes, I'm from Falls Church, Virginia, but originally from Panama."

Things were really cooking now. As I continued to ask more and more questions, getting to know my beautiful friend, I felt very calm and at ease speaking with her. I learned more about her country of origin, profession, and activities she enjoyed. I learned she came to the United States from Panama, enjoyed watching horse races, which I grew to be a big fan of since following the

Kentucky Derby for the past few years.

She worked as a Project Manager at an International development Organization, overseeing projects focused in the Africa region to help raise the standard of living for poorer and underdeveloped areas of the continent. I was eager to learn more and more about her and what she was passionate about.

As the hours passed, we would find ourselves talking in the pitch dark, sitting on the porch that eventually would only encompass us after the others had left or went inside. It didn't matter; the only person I was interested in speaking with was right in front of me, with her cute little nose, dark brown eyes, and attractive lips.

I wanted to spend more time with her, but I knew she didn't live close by. Immediately, I was worried she would dismiss me due to my location, but I needed to give it a shot. As I nervously asked for her number, I could start to see her lips form a smile once she knew my intention. I became more at ease as I could see her reaction to my request.

We exchanged numbers and later planned to meet each other in New York City in a couple weeks. I was so happy to get her number, as I stared at my contacts list on the way home to Brandon's house. This time felt different. It felt like something I hadn't experienced before.

I couldn't wait to talk to her again, which was strange because I rarely felt this way after an initial encounter.

The next morning, on the bus ride back to New York, I texted Liliana and continued to learn more about her. Before I knew it, another four hours had gone by so quickly, but I was intrigued to learn more about her family and past experiences. I curtailed my expectations because I had overcommitted before and it resulted in heartache, but I couldn't stop thinking of her.

When our conversation ended, I sat in my seat thinking, "Could she be someone I have been searching for?" I closed my eyes and visualized the great weekend I had and the intriguing friend I had just made. What a weekend it was.

The first time Liliana and I had met each other since the engagement party in Virginia, we scheduled a quiet weekend together in early September, as she visited me in New York City. She felt comfortable staying in a hotel, since we were just starting our friendship, and agreed that we didn't want to rush into things. It was the first time I had a relationship where we took our time, learned about one another, then built the foundation first, before investing emotions.

I'll always remember the first time we met each

other. She was staying on the east side of Manhattan at the Roosevelt Hotel. I remember being a little nervous as I arrived. I wasn't sure if we would pick up where we left off, or if our great first encounter was an aberration. I hoped she would still enjoy seeing me.

When I first walked in, I immediately saw her from the golden revolving door, standing patiently on the large dark cherry red carpet that led up the white marble staircase and into to the grand lobby. She was as beautiful and elegant as I remembered her to be, as she whisked her long brown hair away from her eyes and smiled when she saw me. I had never seen someone look so pretty. I couldn't believe, in a city of nine million people, the person she was waiting for was me.

We walked up the two sets of stairs and into the grand lobby that included a large diamond chandelier as the centerpiece with large white leather chairs on either side. Off to the left was the lobby bar, which consisted of a long deep brown wooden bar with several people enjoying mixed concoctions or dirty martinis. Around the corner and up the long dark hallway was a private billiard room where you could hear "the break" which would introduce the next highly competitive round of pool. You could see the crystal glasses holding aged scotch, as the cigar smoke swirled around the large private section.

It was something out of a classic movie that would star Marlon Brando and Marilyn Monroe. Approaching the bar on the left, you could see the section that contained four brown leather sofas being encompassed by long dark brown wooden panels, all taking a back seat to the wonderfully painted and golden framed Theodore Roosevelt portrait. The late president stood tall as a strong and confident leader overseeing his welcomed patrons.

The atmosphere was intoxicating as we found a nice secluded table for the two of us. We both enjoyed Bacardi Rum and Coke and discussed what exciting events we had encountered since our two weeks apart. We started to plan out our evening and where we would go to dinner. We had decided to go to Rockefeller Center to see the plaza and continue our rendezvous there.

Later, as we were seated in the far left corner of the Brasserie Ruhlmann restaurant in the Rockefeller plaza, I could see her dark and deep intriguing brown eyes staring back at me as we discussed our weekend's plans. I felt so at ease with her. I hadn't felt this way before. It felt right.

For dinner, I enjoyed the pork chops while she had the almond crusted tilapia. Then we finished off our first dinner together with chocolate lava cake a la mode.

As we left Rockefeller Center and approached Avenue of the Americas, there was a large pool and fountain that displayed the famous red ornaments that were arranged in front of the Exxon Building across from the Radio City Music Hall. There was a long black granite bench surrounding the fountain's four sides.

As we sat down next to each other to people watch, she began to sit a little closer to me. She brushed her hair away from her beautiful face, and I could see her eyes stare back at me. I wanted to kiss her, I believe she wanted to be kissed, but like an idiot, I just smiled back at her. As we sat there a little longer, I put my arm around her to test the waters. She didn't move away, so the green light was clearly being displayed as she made eye contact again. I slowly moved in kissed her cheek. I could hear her quietly giggle.

I slowly kissed her cheek, moving towards my target. As I got closer, I could feel the slight nervous tension between us, but there was no going back now. I was in too deep. I closed my eyes and slightly extended my lips hoping to meet hers. To my relief, there was no hesitation, as I felt her full, sexy lips meet mine. It felt great. It felt like I hoped it would. I didn't feel anyone around us, the city was ours in those moments.

As we walked back to the Roosevelt Hotel, passing

several clothing boutiques on Fifth Avenue, I felt her hand reach out and then tightly clench to mine. I walked her to the golden revolving door and kissed her again for the great evening as we returned to our separate residences for the night. I will always remember that night. I am so glad that she came to visit. The Roosevelt Hotel will always have a special place in my heart as it was the first night I spent with my wife.

We had a wonderful weekend spending the days at Central and Bryant Parks, along with our evenings going out for dinner to a great Peruvian restaurant in the city called Pio Pio where we enjoyed rotisserie style chicken, yellow rice, black beans, and sweet plantains, all covered with a spicy "green sauce" that further perfected the meal.

We would also go to Obao for Thai food the next night that had our soon to be favorite laksa soup that came in a large, white porcelain bowl and contained coconut spicy broth with pasta, pork belly, red onions, basil, and a slight taste of lime juice in every spoonful. We would share steamed shrimp dumplings while enjoying a tall glass of wine and coffee to begin and conclude our private dining experience.

Afterwards, we spent the rest of the evening walking up and down Soho or Greenwich Village, window shopping at all the latest fashion. After the second night, she insisted on residing in her hotel quarters. I could respect this decision as I didn't want to rush and ruin the momentum we had built up over the past couple days. From our initial meeting, I could tell she would be the woman I would bring home to meet my parents.

I could already see the encounter playing out in my mind: how my mother and Lili would enjoy wine and discuss different favorite dishes they enjoyed preparing, while my father and I would entertain ourselves in a spirited conversation regarding the current financial activity or the latest major sporting event, enjoying a mixed drink usually consisting of his personal favorite "Manhattan on the rocks." I didn't want to jump the gun, but in all honesty, that weekend was the time I believed she would be the one. I never felt this way before, so I wasn't completely sure what the tell-tale signs were. I would need to speak with my friend Jay, since he was the only good friend I had that was already married for an extended period of time.

The next morning Lili and I would meet at the ever popular "44 & X" for brunch. I would enjoy the large western omelet, filled with sausage, tomato, onion, and American cheese, while she enjoyed the delicious Huevos Rancheros topped with salsa, sour cream and guacamole.

After enjoying a couple refills of coffee, it was time to take her back to 30th street and 7th avenue, where the noon bus awaited her arrival. After a hug and quick peck on the lips, she was off, heading back towards Virginia/Washington D.C. area. I was sad to see her go, but enjoyed spending time with her. Before I could worry about if we would see her again, I quickly received the text, "I had an amazing weekend with you. I can't wait for you to come visit me in DC in a couple weeks!" I was so excited that I couldn't take the smile off my face for the rest of the day.

It was nice to meet a great person while I was figuring out the city. She came into my life at a perfect time, when I needed her most, as it helped avoid any loneliness that would surely have ensued as the months would go by.

As time passed, our relationship became stronger and after three months we decided to become more exclusive. It felt great to be in a serious relationship, as it had been a few years, and to continue a deeper relationship with the beautiful girl I met on that bright and sunny day in September. I loved being able to express my thoughts and past with her, and without any judgement. It was great finding a supportive listener who I felt comfortable around and could share my innermost thoughts with.

It wasn't long before Lili and my parents scheduled a weekend to meet one another. They would both make their way to New York City, where my parents would stay at a nearby hotel in midtown Manhattan while Lili stayed in my apartment with me. I wasn't worried or concerned about them meeting for the first time as we both came from caring families that revolved around passion for one another and, of course, food.

Lili and I met my parents first for coffee in the morning at a local Starbucks. It was nice to see her embrace my parents for the first time as I could envision a lifetime of these encounters. It was so important to me that my mother and Lili enjoyed each other's company. They were the most important women, along with my sister, in my life. They would become the motivation for me to continue to thrive in life and reach for new heights. They inspired me to be better and expect more out of myself. From that moment, I decided that I would make a promise to them and myself: a promise where I would refuse to let them down. I wanted these special women to be proud of me and nothing would stand in my way of achieving a greater level of success and happiness.

After coffee and a light pastry we were off to Bryant Park, my favorite place to relax and think about life. We found four small green chairs and a table where we sat on the side of the large lawn that overlooked the beautifully white pillared and world famous New York Public Library. Every weekend I would walk from Eighth Avenue to Avenue of the Americas (Sixth Avenue) and sit in a chair residing along the lawn or lay on the grass looking up at the sky. I would do this all day, as I would bring the newspaper and pack a lunch for the several hour stay. Relaxing would help me gain happiness and pleasure by taking time to myself and my thoughts. I would keep reiterating the things I wanted to achieve.

After relaxing and getting to know one another we headed to the wonderful Eataly Italian Marketplace located in the Flatiron District. This is considered the largest Italian marketplace in the world, comprising a variety of restaurants, food and beverage counters, a bakery, cooking school, and large wine bar centrally located in the store. The ladies enjoyed glasses of Pinot Grigio while my father and I selected full bodied glasses of Cabernet Sauvignon. In addition, we enjoyed a large tasting sampler which consisted of a large cutting board that held various cheeses such as asiago and mozzarella, an assortment of green and black olives, and salted meats such as mortadella and prosciutto.

I loved seeing some of the most important people

in my life enjoying a meal together. Family is so important to me and seeing another member being welcomed in to make the dynamic that much stronger and unified, excites and invigorates me. For dinner, we stayed within Eataly enjoying a Margherita pizza to start, then each one of us selecting our favorite pasta dish that included spaghetti Bolognese, linguine pasta with clams and mussels, bowtie pasta with mushroom truffles served in a light cream sauce, and the always popular Lasagna. The night closed with us enjoying espresso and cappuccinos.

The weekend went so quickly, but it was memorable seeing the love of my life being welcomed with open arms by my parents. They could see how happy I was. The time spent with my parents only reassured me that the one I would choose to marry was welcomed and respected by the two people in my family that I care most about.

Lili and I would go on to visit each other two weekends a month, rotating trips between Virginia/ Washington DC and New York City, as we continued our relationship. The long five hour bus rides were difficult at times, where feeling would be certainly lost in the lower extremities. Still, it felt great to share holidays with her, especially when we prepared our first Thanksgiving turkey with all the sides.

I knew early on that she would be the one I would propose to. I would visualize the day I would get on one knee and express my love for her. My search would be over and my long lasting relationship with "the one" would begin. I continued to visualize looking into her eyes, putting myself completely in her hands, to decide if she believed in what we had as much as I did.

I remember talking to my good friend Jay at the historic Big Tree Inn a few years earlier. The popular bar was located next to the Buffalo Bills stadium in Orchard Park, where NFL Legends such as Jim Kelly and Dan Marino would meet the night before and in the late afternoon after their historic matchups during the nineteen nineties.

I asked Jay, who I had played with on the Buffalo Hornets team for three years and at Saint Francis High School for four years, how he knew that his wife was the one.

He calmly replied after putting down his pint of beer, "You'll just know man, you'll know." He winked back with a sense of pride in his response.

I politely replied back, "Thanks for nothing bud." What kind of answer was that? That didn't help, it didn't tell me what signs to look out for or what I would need to hear from Lili to know she was the one. God, I needed to get new friends.

After going through the process on my own, and looking back on that brief conversation, you know what? Jay was right. There isn't a sign or a word that you will hear that tells you she's the one. It's a gut feeling—it's intuition, that's what it is. That's how you know: by trusting your instincts and being in tune and fully aware of how you feel when that person is near and the moments you share with them. Of course, "You'll just know" works too. I would later share another pint with my old and good friend and thanked him for his wisdom, as we shared a good laugh as we reminisced about our original conversation.

CHAPTER 10:
LAW OF ATTRACTION
AND SUCCESS PRINCIPLES

"You meet your must my friends. Maybe it's time to change your musts. Some people's musts are to survive. Some people's musts are to be OK. Some people's musts are to have freedom. Some people's musts are to have more money than they can possibly spend. Some people's musts are to take care of everyone around them. Whatever your must is, you're going to get it. Think how your life would be different, if you raised the standard of what you expected from yourself, not your people, but of yourself, to that level. How things could shift. It's all about changing your shoulds to musts. It all about going back and saying this is how it's going to be."

—Tony Robbins

As Liliana and I continued to date, along with my experience at Citi occurring simultaneously, she started to sense the stresses at work were starting to weigh on me. I was becoming more and more negative in regards to my work situation, and it was starting to take a toll on how I was perceiving the world around me. I was becoming too pessimistic and my circumstances were continuing to drain and even depress me.

One of the best gifts she shared with me, that has changed my life forever, was a small book called "The Secret." This paperback book was one of the most powerful books I had ever read. It helped me to remain strong and keep perspective, along with securing a positive attitude while I was enduring life at work.

It taught me, through the "law of attraction," that there is a connected relationship we all have with the Universe. More specifically, it taught me that I had complete control over my life, instead of feeling that I was helpless at the hands of my experiences. It taught me that through my innermost thoughts and feelings that I could create the person I wanted me to be and the future I wanted to enjoy.

Once I started to read, I couldn't get enough, as I flew through the pages until completion. I was starving for direction and purpose in my life. I needed to start putting the law of attraction powers to work and with a more concentrated focus. I would quickly reread the paperback, and immediately started trying to implement the concepts into my mind on a daily routine. The extremely influential and gifted speakers that graced the pages of what would become my new "creed" were so gifted and inspiring with their words. These inspirational people included Jack Canfield, Michael Bernard Beckwith, John Assaraf, and Lisa Nichols to name a few.

As I began reading, I quickly learned that I needed to view myself as a magnet: that what I am, I have attracted to myself. All the events in my life, whether triumphs in playing Hockey or tribulations consisting of my ruptured spleen, and alcohol addiction, I have been brought to me by my thoughts, beliefs, feelings, and—of course—actions. If I am negative, I will receive negativity coming back to me, from other people, events, or results achieved. The same concept applies if I am positive; I will receive positive events and results being manifested back to me.

What a simple concept, but many people, including myself, do not focus or concentrate on this behavior with their conscious mind. I immediately started applying this to my everyday life. I would help older people get onto the subway, help pull their grocery cart up a slight incline if they struggled, or get up of my seat for them to sit down. I would pick up an item if someone dropped it and return it to them, or simply display a brief smile to someone that was having a rough morning.

I immediately started seeing the positive results reflecting back to me, as I would start to receive the same type of behavior from total strangers or colleagues at work at Bloomberg. I would start to receive soup, coffee, or even Friday afternoon ice cream from colleagues without having to ask. I would receive compliments on my work attire or a simple smile being returned back to me. After enough of these reactions, I started to change my mindset and perceptions of my environment. What a powerful tool at the most basic level, but it works and it helped me feel better about my circumstances. Work was even more pleasant along with the ride home on the sometimes unbearably hot subway. It was helping my day to day life become much more tolerable and easier to manage.

While applying this concept to my life, I also started to implement the three step process of "ask, believe, and receive" where I would make a request to the Universe, believe not only that I deserved it and that it would manifest, but to also firmly believe that I already had it. The last step was having my request come to fruition.

It felt uncomfortable at first asking subconsciously or looking at the sky asking the Universe to listen to my request, but after enough practice it became second nature as I continued to focus on the goals and positive outcomes I wanted to experience. It was easy to believe that I deserved it, after the life events I had gone through, but it was extremely difficult for me to believe in having things that I couldn't readily observe.

After enough practice and visualizing having the objects in my mind, I would start to see them appear. I started off small, like a glass of water or cup of coffee. I would remain still and picture the cup or glass that held the beverage, the look of the clear water or the dark brown Arabica coffee beans filling the cup. I would concentrate on the humming and hissing sounds of the coffee machine as it prepared to make the next cup. I would visualize feeling the hot beverage as it hit my lips and the potent liquid as it went down my throat and into my stomach. I would concentrate and focus on receiving that cup of coffee while I started my day at work and how good it felt to receive. I would picture myself walking up to the machine, hearing the wonderful sounds of the machine, and smelling the fresh ground coffee beans made just for me, right before I took my first sip. I noticed that the coffee started to taste even more wonderful than usual by the simple mental visualization techniques I was instilling into my mind.

I would continue to work on other items, such as my sandwich consisting of turkey and avocado on a potato bun for lunch, as the behavior became more and more practiced and eventually routine.

I also learned about the powerful concept of truly feeling grateful for what I currently had. This would help speed up the process of the Universe delivering my request to me in reality. I would find myself, as I woke up or laid in bed, consistently reiterating in my mind the things I was grateful for.

I was grateful for the wonderful and supportive family that I was born into, where many others may not be able to say the same. I was happy and blessed to have met Liliana after so many failed relationships. I was blessed to have the opportunity to move to New York City and live in such an amazing place. The list went on and on, from my passion in finance, job security and pleasant co-workers at Bloomberg, to having enough money to save in such an expensive area, and being grateful to have known and shared so many great memories with my grandparents.

As I continued to read on, there were more important topics discussed which focused around different concepts such as money, relationships, and health. I would read more in-depth into these areas and the internal struggle most people had with one or all of these aspects. The book dove into the power of visualization, by seeing things as though I already had them.

To help with this process and help my mind focus, I would need to be in a state of relaxation and tranquility. The book suggested meditation as a helpful way to achieve this state of mind. Digging deeper into visualization, I would write down in detail the things I wanted to achieve as though I already had them, while displaying gratitude for having received all the things I had in my life.

In addition to the writing process, I would create a "vision board," which is a collage of pictures of things that I wanted to receive, whether it was a material object or experience that I would want to enjoy such as traveling or lifestyle. Most importantly, if this behavior was sustained for a long enough period of time, say a month or two depending on the person, it would breed confidence and provide the reader with the internal power to go after their dreams.

On my vision board I had pictures of a beautiful stone mansion with an Infiniti pool located in a remote area of Venice, a picture of a silver Lamborghini Montreal, various pictures of Rome, Venice, and the Amalfi coast, a picture of a white Leer Jet, a diamond encrusted Rolex, and lastly a picture of Muhammad Ali surrounded by stacks upon stacks of money that symbolized wealth and success.

With everything that was happening at work, this book came into my life at the right time, as it helped me realize I had the power to change things. It helped me stand up for myself and say enough to the constant ridicule. It helped me fight back where normally, in a workplace setting, I would be "professional" and take the abuse.

I needed to put an end to that type of impact on my life as it was weighing on me. I am extremely grateful Liliana showed me "The Secret." After the work conflict came to a successful resolution, I started to think about what else this powerful book could do for me.

I read the book again, cover to cover, and focused upon the section regarding money, health and relationships. Having been blessed with good health and a strong relationship with Liliana and my family, I put all of my focus on the money section. Before anyone starts to draw conclusions, let me explain why I chose the money part to put my focus and efforts towards.

My main reason for putting my focus towards money is first and foremost for myself, because I want to prove to myself that I have the talent and ability to become a millionaire. As a direct result of achieving that status, I will be able to take care of my wife and her parents, our children someday, and my parents, sister, and her children.

These people are the nucleus that means everything in the world to me. I want to show them a higher level in this life that is full of abundance, prosperity, and wealth. I don't want them to go without or not be able to experience everything this beautiful life has to offer. Most importantly, I want to reward them for believing in me and sticking by me through the surgery, through the alcohol issues, through the pain, through the sadness that I caused everyone.

What drives me is the power of redemption. I wasn't put on this earth to be average, to live in peddling mediocrity, and to put my love ones through pain because of my actions. I want to reward the ones I love by helping them see the great things in life and help inspire them to raise their expectations for themselves.

I want my grandparents to look down from heaven and be proud of what they see, and I want to be able to look at myself in the mirror and know that I set out a goal and I obtained it. I have put myself through a personal hell to the point where it could have cost me my life twice, and I cannot do that to myself or my family again.

I have run out of chances. I must be fully accountable. I will be the one that is solely responsible for taking

my family out of their current status and help them realize the better life they've always wanted for themselves.
I want to realize the better life that I have dreamt about
for years, but was too afraid to take the risks necessary
for my "dream scenario" to manifest. The past is done, all
I can do is learn from it, but it would not hold me back
anymore. It would instead be the driving force for my
future.

"The secret" was the foundation, the core of my
belief system, but that was just the beginning. To further
help focus my mind on this lofty but achievable goal, I
would begin a nightly routine of hour-long meditation.

At first, it felt strange to sit in silence; I had come
from a very active childhood that hadn't quite ever
stopped. After a while, as I continued to practice meditation, my mind would be still and thoughts became
clearer and clearer, more and more vivid.

I could see the large stacks of money, neatly sorted
and compact, with large, tight rubber bands that kept
them in place: stacks upon stacks as far back as the eye
could see. I would pick two stacks off the pile and bring
them directly into my view. The large stacks of money
were nearly organized, securely located on a large metal
table placed inside of a bank's safety deposit room.

I could see the top $100 bills that had Benjamin

Franklin's face displayed across the middle. I could see myself clapping the stacks together, being astonished by how heavy they were, and loving the thud sound they would make as the stacks came together. I could hear the whishing sounds of dollar bills as I ran my finger across the top, feeling each dollar bill grace my finger tip. After holding the large, heavy stacks, I would return them back to the metal table and just stand there, taking in the feelings of accomplishing what I saw before me.

Next, I would picture myself on an airport runway, walking with my wife and child towards our private Leer Jet. I was wearing a custom made and perfectly tailored blue suit. As I walked towards the few stairs that led into the aircraft, my attention would go directly to the diamond encrusted Rolex on my left wrist that was hiding underneath my sleeve.

My focus would then go onto my ring finger that displayed a gold and rose gold wedding band. This was not just any wedding band, but the wedding band my grandfather wore for over 40 years of marriage. My attention would then go up towards my hand where I could see the knuckles, veins, fingernails, and hair on my wrist.

My hand was tightly holding an object that I would turn over to see my palm, displaying the Chinese "wealth" good luck charm. I could see the diamond and gold encrusted charm that was attached to a yellow string that was tightly wound around my wrist.

My focus and my attention would now be directed on the right hand, as it pulled me up the metal stairs leading into the aircraft. Step by step up the small flight of stairs, I could see my white Bruno Magli shoes leading the way. As I peered into the aircraft and my focus would come off my shoes to eye level, I was greeted by the pilot that would be taking us on our trip.

I shook his hand as he asked me, "Are you excited to surprise your parents and show them Europe?" I politely nodded to confirm that I was ready. My beautiful Panamanian wife was right behind me in a dark blue dress holding our newborn child. As we directed ourselves to our white leather captain seats, which directly faced one another, I could see my wife whispering to me, mouthing the words "I love you."

Before I could react and become emotional, I could hear the voices of my parents as they climbed aboard, confused on why they were being directed onto a private jet by the stewardess. It all made sense to them when they saw my face, with a large grin that stretched from ear to ear.

They climbed aboard, one by one—my mother, my father, my sister, her husband, my adorable little nephews, my in-laws. I would hug and kiss my mother, mother in law, and sister. I would firmly shake the hands of my father, father in law and brother in law that I looked up to and admired. I could feel the strong force and pressure as my hands would create a firm grip with theirs.

Lastly would come my nephews. I picked them both up at the same time, so I could show them a view six feet and one inch off the ground and have them join me at eye level. I gave them a strong hug and multiple kisses on their cheeks, until they requested to be put down.

Once everyone was seated, I stood in front of the group, thanking them for the support and motivation they had provided me over the time I had known them and revealed to them our two week excursion being split evenly between the cities of Barcelona and Venice. As their eyes lit up, I would give the pilot the nod to begin our ascendance into the clear blue skies.

I would then take my seat, seeing my wife and child directly in front of me and my family to the right as they were discussing the itineraries provided to them and the everlasting smiles on their faces. I would then turn my attention to the clear window displaying the runway as we began our takeoff. I could hear the engine start to hum, gaining strength and ferocity. Then we began to move, faster and faster we went to gain the appropriate speed for takeoff. As the tires left the tarmac, we continued to gain altitude more and more quickly; the tears of joy would roll down my cheeks and into the short brown facial hairs on my lower cheeks and mouth. I had fulfilled my dream, I had manifested my goal. In short, I had turned my "shoulds" into "musts."

I had the vision, but to that point, I had not manifested anything into my life. Was this secret real or just a hoax? The more and more I concentrated on this dream, after a few weeks things started to happen. The first occurrence was at the ATM machine located right in front of my building.

It was early Saturday morning, about 8 AM, and I was heading out to get my cup of coffee to start my day. I had always looked at the ATM, imagining one day there would be money waiting just for me. This morning, as I looked at the machine, there was something in the there.

I stormed into the little pizza shop that had the ATM and I went right for the object. I quickly took out my bank card, so it didn't look like I was flying towards the ATM. As I looked down there was a crisp twenty-dollar bill there. "How cool," I thought to myself. As I went to pick up the twenty dollar bill, I noticed there were more underneath it. One by one, I kept seeing more twenty dollar bills. I couldn't believe it. I scooped them all up and panned them out.

There were five. That's one hundred dollars, the same hundred dollars that I had seen on the stacks, which I had been meditating about for weeks. I was blown away. Nothing like this had ever happened to me until this point. This could just be a coincidence, although I didn't think so.

A few days later at work, while I was walking towards the elevator, the person walking past me a few feet away dropped money on the ground. The moment the money left his pocket, my mind was locked in. Of a floor full of people, I was the only person who saw and acted on it. As I quickly approached the dollar bill I noticed it was not a twenty-dollar bill, but a one hundred dollar bill. I picked it up and my mind went crazy, as I knew this is what I had been visualizing: money coming to me quickly and easily.

After a few moments of excitement, cooler heads prevailed. I quickly chased him down around the corner and returned the money to the rightful owner. He was so relieved when he saw me present the lost bill to him.

For a few minutes after giving it back, my mind punished me for returning the money. I could hear the internal struggle going on. On one side I could hear,

"How could you give back the money? This is what you wanted, what you visualized about for so long, how could you?" On the other side, I could hear, "You did the right thing, he would have dearly missed the money, you should feel good about what you have done." Overall, the good side of my brain, who thought I did something noble by returning the money, dominated my emotions. I left the day feeling better about what I had done.

Lili had recently relocated from Virginia to New York City, and we had just moved into our new two-bed-room apartment in Astoria. The first weekend there, Lili and I came home from dinner and saw our mail sitting on the stairs. Walking up the stairs and into the kitch-en, I went through the mail to a few wedding invitation responses and saw that even though two invitations were from couples who could not attend, both of them gave one hundred dollar checks as a gift to the wedding.

I immediately thought I was being rewarded for the good deed I had done just two days prior and then some. If that wasn't enough, four days later a manager at work who heard about my engagement bought me a bottle of champagne worth, you guessed it, one hundred dollars. I couldn't believe this; it was incredible.

Then another few days later, as Lili and I came home from the park, there laid a bottle of champagne from the neighbors below us, along with a beautiful note welcoming us to the building. I was blown away by the acts of kindness since I had started the journey of recognizing the Universe's power and impact on my life. From my own personal experiences, the law of attraction does indeed work. I couldn't wait for what else the Universe had in store for me, since I had learned how to use the law and was grateful for its powers.

The vision was firmly implanted into my mind, and I was seeing results of things coming to me, but I had to start focusing harder on achieving my "dream scenario." I knew my end goal, but now I needed to discover what actions I would take for this dream to become reality. I had never done this process before and needed confidence to take the necessary actions. I was looking for a powerful message that I could grasp in regards to taking action. I found it in "The Secret" with the powerful quote from Martin Luther King Jr. as he stated: "Take the first step in faith. You don't have to see the whole staircase. Just take the first step." This is exactly what I needed to hear. Just take action step by step, eventually getting to the end goal.

So as a result, I started to write down the changes I wanted to create in my life to achieve my "dream scenario" and what actions I was going to take to make these changes manifest.

I thought about what brought me the most joy in my life and what I wanted to own to have the life that I wanted. I knew I wanted to be a millionaire, but I needed to dig deeper into what I loved doing and generate a list. My goals that I wanted to achieve included creating a skating school for young hockey players who had intermediate and advanced level skills, own a two bedroom rental property in Panama's historic "Casco Viejo" district, move out of my alcove studio and into a two bedroom apartment in New York City for the same amount I was paying now, then working towards home ownership, becoming an Account Manager at work, and lastly and most passionately, helping to inspire people who have had fallen on difficult times due to dramatic life- changing events. I would do this through attending group meetings and presenting my story to different care groups for people who needed to hear my story. Lastly, I needed to provide them my story and lessons I had learned as a blueprint on how they could change their lives. I would accomplish this by writing a book. I had a unique story to tell. It's about time the world heard it.

An important aspect that I have learned over time is that the relationship a person has with their mind or inner voice and how this understanding it is very important when trying to achieve goals. As Denzel Washington once said as he met with young children at the Boys and Girls Club in Brooklyn, NY: "True desire in the heart, for anything good, is God's proof to you, sent beforehand, to indicate that it's yours already. You already have it. Claim it!" He would go on to say "Dreams without goals, remain dreams. Goals, on the road to achievement, are accomplished by discipline and consistency." I love this quote because it creates the right mindset to go after big dreams. I feel most people want to achieve wealth to either have financial security or have the ability to improve their current life or surroundings by being able to do what they love to do. I believe money magnifies the person for what they truly are. That is why the intention behind wanting wealth and success is so important.

I also believe a lack of confidence or doubt creates emotions of fear that keeps the common person from taking action. This is because I feel the common person is not consciously aware of the critical relationship of how their emotions and internal relationship drives their behaviors. The great thing is that anyone, with enough practice and awareness, can change the way they think, process, and behave when faced with obstacles keeping them from their goals. People can deter themselves with their thoughts, constantly reinforcing these limiting beliefs on what or how much they can accomplish. For me, I noticed how in the past my negative mindset would prevent me from achieving personal goals of mines, such as making more money or obtaining the next promotion. My fear of failure was greater than my drive for success. By lacking the necessary confidence, I was falling short of accomplishing the goals I focused and dreamed about. I was constantly receiving what I dreaded, instead of focusing on what I desired. Once I learned and understood how the mind works, and how easy it is to change your responses to favorable results, I began to see positive changes impacting my life. As a result, these positive outcomes further developed my change in lifestyle and behavior. I refused to get stuck on the past or feeling of uncertainty, but instead, use those thoughts and feelings to fuel myself forward, take action, and keep myself moving towards the goal I have set.

I feel our beliefs come from our environment: our friends, our family, our parents, the television shows we watch, the books we read, and the music we listen to. Depending on what you have been told growing up or past failures you have experienced, I feel it keeps the average person from attempting or pushing through when things get hard or difficult.

When I tried to change the way I thought and

strengthen my faith and belief in my ability to create things, I knew I needed to condition my brain to trust what I was telling it. From personal experiences, it can be very difficult for your brain to believe and accept the messages, if in the past you have not kept your word on past promises or agreements you have made. I feel that after enough broken promises, the harder it will be to change your mindset because you have conditioned your brain not to trust what you're promising.

In my life, I was good at keeping promises with myself, but what I lacked was the confidence and faith in things I could not see. That was the hardest part of this entire process for me was believing I had things that I could not see right in front of my own eyes. It took six months of meditation and constant reinforcement of the following phrase to train my brain. "You get it when you believe it. You get it when you believe you have it." I learned this phrase from an Oprah Interview that was conducted with actor Jim Carey. This phrase motivated my mind to trust and have faith that things I desired would appear as long as I believed I already had them. This was such a foreign concept to me, believing of having things I couldn't see, as my mind struggled to comprehend and truly believe this concept. After enough constant focus on the concept, I started to believe and after a few more months, I had mastered it. I would focus and dwell on the feeling it gave me, having millions of dollars and manifesting my "dream scenario". The feeling would get stronger and stronger as the more actions I would take towards the goals I had set for myself. As a result, it was getting easier and easier to train my brain and have it believe the thoughts I was forcing into my conscious mind through consistent repetition.

As mentioned before, the change was not im-mediate. It took time and dedication for it to become a habit, which in turn, resulted in a belief. Every small development or action taken, strengthened my belief system when focused on the larger goal. I would take small bites or small actions until I was able to consume or achieve the entire goal. It was also important that I believed that the way would come or be shown to me. I didn't worry about how I was going to achieve the goal. It was a foregone conclusion that I would succeed and that there was no other possible outcome as I continued to take action. The fear of failing no longer existed as I kept myself accountable on a daily basis. Every morning when I woke up, I would ask myself "How bad do you want this? What are you willing to do for this to become a reality?" My answer was and has always been, "I want this with all my heart and all my soul and I am willing to

do whatever it takes for my dream scenario be a reality."
This was my way of keeping myself in check, and keeping
focus or perspective on what my larger goal was. It was
also a way of keeping myself focused on who I was going
to help and reward when the ultimate prize had materialized. I made my goals "must haves" and fully understood
the promise and responsibility I had to myself and those I
would help. Failure, giving up, and quitting were simply
not options. I was going to see this through.

Chapter 11:
Off To Bloomberg

"When a seed is planted in the ground, all you can do is water it. You cannot control the sunshine, you cannot control the weather, you cannot control what locusts will come and try to destroy it. All you can do is plant your seed into the ground, water it, and believe. That is what got me to this position that I am in right now. I would not stop believing!"

—Tyler Perry

After the decision was made to leave Citi for a fresh start and career growth, it was clear I still wanted to stay within the financial sector. I have always had an interest in finance and in the ever-changing markets.

I had been in the banking industry for the majority of my career—five years to be exact—but I was ready for a new perspective. I wanted to expand and enhance my client-facing experience. I wanted to go to a place that was well known in the city and had a solid reputation in the market place.

I chose Bloomberg. I was so happy when they first replied to my application to set up an interview date to discuss supporting their buy side trading solution. It matched my past experience in banking, gave me more knowledge of the Bloomberg Terminal, and it would expand my working knowledge of the buy side hedge funds and wealth management companies in the United States and Canada.

When I first stepped into the 731 Lexington Avenue building, I was completely blown away by the beautifully modern twenty-nine floor global headquarters. It was everything I had hoped for in an office building as it also housed retail outlets, high-end restaurants and 105 luxury condominiums.

The sky scraper filled a full city block between Lexington and Third Avenues on 59th Street. The complex featured two towers constructed above a steel office and retail section, separated by a seven-story atrium. I hadn't landed the job yet, but I was hooked the moment I stepped inside as I walked through the entrance and headed down the long corridor that included glacier like stalactites along the right-hand side wall.

Heading towards the elevators, that would light up in green and red to display elevators that were going up and down, were referenced to display the colors of a bull or bear market. As I headed up to the 6th floor atrium, the building opened up to include numerous large fish tanks, pantries that included snacks, soft drinks, candy, and tea/coffee stations that served ready to make espresso, cappuccino, and latte.

The walls to my left and right were all glass, which allowed me to peer out and see midtown Manhattan as far as the eye could see in either direction. There were doors located at the four corners of the room that led to four large outside patios for employees to relax and view the surrounding city in a much more up-close and personal way. Across the ceiling was a state of the art message board, summarizing the day's main events and the day's gain or loss on major global stock indexes.

As I sat on the large pink couch, patiently awaiting for my HR representative to greet me, I was anxious and excited to get started. This was where I wanted to be, and this was where I wanted to take my career on the next step in my journey.

I would go through two separate days of interviews, meeting my eventual Team Leaders, Managers, Directors, and Global Heads. I had a great conversation with them all and felt comfortable there even though I hadn't started yet. In the interviews we discussed my past working experiences, my strengths and weaknesses, my product knowledge of certain financial products, my view of current legislation and market movements, where I felt the market would go next, and what I brought as an asset to the company. At the end of the final interview, I met with the HR person, who walked me down the glass stairs and back towards the elevators. I didn't want to leave. How many places could you say that about?

I headed back towards the ground floor, returning my badge that allowed me clearance for the day. I had a good feeling as I walked towards the revolving doors that led outside to the awaiting Bloomingdales department store. Two days later, I received the call I was hoping for: the next phase of my career would begin at Bloomberg.

I would begin at a two-day orientation that explained the company culture and high level functionality of the Bloomberg terminal. After a month of reading product learning courses, and proactively taking part in daily responsibilities, it was time for my two-week intensive training.

Here I would learn the buy-side system that I would support and develop an in depth knowledge of the system and the settings that would impact user functionality. During this time, I was so fortunate that I met a colleague named Alex. He was highly intelligent, hardworking, and gifted when it came to networking, but his strongest attribute was his compassion. While others were too busy in their day to day responsibilities, he took the time to help, explain, and guide others.

He would soon move on to Account Management, but his ability to relate to and communicate with me was invaluable. As I would move along in my first year, I used my knowledge from the banking industry and produced two in-depth PowerPoints of swap workflow.

I wasn't asked to do this. I wanted to give back to the team I was supporting since many didn't understand the product or the workflow. I spent many hours after work in the evening perfecting those presentations, and was honored to present to the group what I had gained over my five years and connect knowledge to the work-flow used at Bloomberg.

I was fortunate enough through networking to be introduced to a fellow Buffalonian named Chris. Chris went to the University of Rochester then moved to New York City around the same age that I did. He was mar-ried to a wonderful woman and was the father of two beautiful children. He was the Team Leader for Account Management that had supported premium clients for the past seven years.

We immediately had a common bond, based on

the sports teams we supported and—more importantly—the town that we grew up in. I felt like I had known
him my whole life, as he understood the roots that I had
developed from. We would meet up and root for the
Buffalo Bills and Sabres when they would play against
the other New York teams such as the Jets, Rangers, and
Islanders. We enjoyed thrilling sporting events at MetLife
Stadium, the Barclays Center, and the famous Madison
Square Garden.

   He was very wise and offered guidance to achieve
both short term and long term goals, but to not lose
myself or my morals in the process. I never had a mentor
before in my working career, as I learned everything the
hard way through making mistakes and persevering, but
it was nice to have finally met such a great person after
my long journey. He provided valuable advice not only
about work and how to get where I wanted to end up
career wise, which was to be an Account Manager under
his guidance, but also about life where balancing personal goals and the goals between Lili and I were so important for a healthy and loving marriage. He was someone
whose advice I could trust and rely on.

   While working at both Citi and at Bloomberg for
a combined three years, I was staying in the same alcove
studio apartment, which had become cramped. I needed

to focus on taking the next step in my life. I knew Liliana was the one for me, as she loved and supported my new focus and goals unconditionally. I could never thank her enough for bringing "The Secret" into my life, as it provided the subtle nudge to finally think about the well-being of others and begin writing this story.

As the first few months turned into two wonderful years, I knew it was time for that all-important purchase. I wanted to show her my gratitude for sticking by me and forcing me to change my outlook and perspective on life and my surroundings. I wanted to thank her for giving her number two years earlier to a man struggling to find his way and breathing new life into his heart, mind, and soul.

One day, I would be able to tell her how much she meant to me and how much I needed her. I'd be able to tell her that she was the only true girlfriend I ever had or ever wanted. One day, I would be able to get on one knee, look into the eyes of the mother of my unborn children, and ask her to intertwine her hopes, dreams, and faith with mine.

I mustered up most of my savings at the time, went to the local jewelry store and found a beautiful 1.5 carat diamond ring that combined gold and rose gold to form the band. I knew she liked more exotic things, so I took a chance on the style, hoping that she would love the gift I was going to propose to her with.

I wasn't sure how I would ask, but I was certain she was the one I would ask. As the summer was rapidly approaching, I remembered the Kentucky Derby would soon be upon us. She grew up with horses, as her family partially owned a Panamanian Triple Crown winner. I had developed an intense bond with the sport after several years of watching, hoping, and praying to one day witness a Triple Crown Winner on American soil.

The day I would propose lined up with my mental timeline, so I decided that the evening of the Kentucky Derby would be the day. Where would I do this? What would be the actual spot for when I would ask? I reminisced about the happiest times I had spent with her—all the dinners, walks in the park, and staying up late in Virginia catching a hot cup of coffee at our favorite place called "Mom and Pop" in the area of Dunnloring.

Only one moment jumped out at me: the Roosevelt Hotel, when I met my wife for the first time in New York. I'll always remember how beautiful she looked standing on the lobby stairs, peering out at me as I entered. I would replay that moment over and over in my head. That hotel was our spot. I also knew she loved Central Park at the famous cast-iron Bow Bridge that overlooked the massive lake, which was one of the most romantic settings and was dead center of the world renowned park.

I had to come up with a plan so we both enjoyed the experience. I got it. I would re-create our first evening, beginning at the Roosevelt Hotel and ending at Bow Bridge in Central Park. As "Derby Day" approached, I could feel the butterflies filling my stomach. I knew she would say yes, but I wanted the moment to be special for her and something we would look back on forever.

A couple days before the special day, I cleverly mentioned going out to watch the Derby and maybe even grab some food.

She quickly replied, "Okay, that sounds fine," in a carefree manner. That was harmless, as it wouldn't sound off any alarms. I was so happy for her to experience the special moment and know that I wanted to commit to her hopes and dreams. I knew she grew up as a little girl dreaming of the day she would put on her wedding dress and walk down the aisle towards the man that cared for her. I was honored to be that person for her.

I knew she wanted something special and thoughtful when the moment I would ask, so I wanted to make sure she loved my idea. The day of the event I mentioned in passing that we may go out for a fancy dinner, so she should make sure she looked her best. I could see her eyebrows raise at my request, and she asked, "How fancy?" with a grin.

Her eagerness quickly dissipated when I replied, "Don't get too excited, it's not that fancy." Smart thinking on my part. I would not tell her where we would watch the race, just that we would go and watch, have a drink, then head to a nice restaurant afterwards. We had gone out for nice dinners before, so she would believe that—so far so good.

She would frequently ask throughout the morning where I would like to go, but I would play nonchalant mentioning anywhere would be acceptable. I could see she was starting to get impatient, as I thought to myself, "Hold on baby, just a few more hours."

As the noon hour turned into the late afternoon, closing in on the 6:30 PM race time, I knew we had to start our trip. We had a lot of ground to cover as we would go to Roosevelt Hotel, Rockefeller Center, and Central Park in one evening. I needed enough time to not feel rushed, and enjoyed the night. It would be chilly out so I carried a light blue spring jacket, in which I would hide the ring box.

That evening we started off on our journey, heading east from Times Square to Madison Avenue. We hopped into the waiting cab, where I quickly described the coordinates of our first destination, the Roosevelt Hotel, by stating to the cab driver, "45th and Madison please."

Lili quickly glanced at me with a puzzled look as if that was a familiar spot she had visited before, but quickly brushed off the hunch. I could see her mind starting to process. As we approached the beautifully historic luxury hotel first opened in 1924, she started to look outside through both side windows and said, "I love this area."

I knew this very well and decided to have the driver drop us off a little bit earlier, so she wouldn't know right away. Once we were only a couple steps away, she noticed the "Roosevelt Hotel" entrance sign. She turned to me and had a huge smile on her face as if this would be the perfect spot to enjoy the race. In that moment, I saw the same beautiful smile that I had seen two years earlier standing on those lobby steps.

As we walked in, beginning to retrace our exact steps, she reached out her hand to hold mine. It was the happiest I had ever seen her. At that moment, I knew she felt something was up, since it was only the second time we had visited this location. As we sat down at the bar and enjoyed our rum and cokes, we would discuss the favorites to win the race.

We didn't know much about the participants, but

as they lined up we immediately agreed on the 3-1 odd horse that had beautiful dark brown skin and was dressed in a light purple cloth that covered the saddle and head gear, only revealing his eyes and ears.

It was a beautiful horse. Then we heard the announcer say, "Next up with 3-1 odds is American Pharaoh." We cheered for the horse we had never heard of, but had a catchy name. A few minutes later, our pick would win the race as we cheered him on as he entered the final furlong and into the final stretch.

After enjoying the race and the perfectly mixed drinks, we left the hotel with such pride after our lucky horse had won, heading towards Rockefeller Center. We quietly strolled up Madison Avenue passing Bryant Park, on our way towards the breathtaking St. Patrick's Cathedral.

Once there, we were only steps away from our second stop of the night, as we would head down towards ground level where the restaurant and lounge area resided. We sat down on a white plush love seat located directly in front of the famous "Prometheus" sculpture, enjoying the panoramic view of colorful flags surrounding us, representing countries from around the world as they flapped in the breeze on a cool summer's night. Looking up at the famous "Thirty Rock" building as it towered overhead seventy stories high, we admired the breathtaking American Art Deco skyscraper as the white lights fully displayed its slim and expressive form.

I was tired from carrying the coat all evening, so I quietly placed it on the couch we shared, under a light red throw pillow with the arms draped over the pocket so she wouldn't see the precious gift that was inside.

I was only a minute away as I headed to the bar quickly ordering our round of drinks. I turned back towards our table, with drinks in tow, and my stomach immediately sank as I saw Lili. She was wearing my coat.

I quickly put the drinks down and forced the coat off of her as I declared, "It's cold, I need my coat." She knew I was acting weird and slightly put off, as I am always warm, but I didn't want to ruin the surprise. After finishing our mojitos, we headed across the street towards our famous spot along the black granite bench. This was a special place since it was where we shared our first kiss. Aww!

After visiting each spot, I would ask her why that particular location was special, and she knew the answer. A perfect three for three. As we sat there watching people as they passed, I felt just as nervous and excited as I did the first time we kissed.

I put my arm around her, rubbing her shoulders,

217

as she was becoming cold. There was no way I would give up my coat, so this was the best I could do. I slowly leaned in for our romantic kiss.

That kiss felt like the culmination of the time we had spent together traveling back and forth from Virginia to New York City. We would no longer be in a long distance relationship; we would begin the next leg of our journey together.

Looking at my watch, I saw that it was almost nine o'clock and it was time we moved onto the last leg of our trip. As we began to get tired from the walking, we took a cab to our fourth and final location, the Bow Bridge. As we approached the side entrance to the park, we walked amongst the beautifully lit "Strawberry Fields" that pay tribute to the late great Beatle, John Lennon.

It was now officially night time, as the park glistened with bright white lights that created the perfect scene. My plan was right on schedule—nothing could stop me now. As we got out of the cab and walked towards the middle of the park, she kept looking back at me. She knew at this point, as I could feel her hand clenching tighter to mine.

It was still exciting. Once she saw the bridge, or what is sometimes referred to as "the symphony of stone," she pulled my arm to hurry up. From a distance, it was perfect: no one was on the bridge and lights were strung across the bridge to display the exquisite Victorian architecture.

It seemed like the bridge and surrounding lake were decorated just for us. I was so grateful for the opportunity that had unfolded. I didn't want to propose in front of a lot of people, and look at my luck—there was no one there. As we approached the side of the bridge, walking along the banks of the lake, I saw a large green sign.

Uh-oh, that couldn't be good. As I got up nice and close I read the sign that stated, "Closed for bridge reconstruction." I was devastated for her. My plan was ruined. We walked all this way, traveled without any issue, and construction was going to do me in.

She looked disappointed, but I quickly noticed to the right, two large cherry blossom trees that had lights hung throughout, unveiling its fully displaying the beautiful pedals. She had lived in the Virginia/Washington D.C. area, and we enjoyed going to the park overlooking the Washington Monument where the rows of several cherry blossom trees were on full display.

This could work—who was I kidding? It *had* to work. We saw a group of girls standing in front of the trees taking selfies. I directed Lili to the nearest park bench as we would look at the stars and discuss our nights events. All the while, I was impatiently looking back at the girls, waiting for them to leave.

It felt like eternity, but just when I was about to stand up and say something, they quickly ran away to their next favorite spot. This was my chance. It was now or never. I couldn't wait for the bridge to be repaired.

I directed Lili to the beautiful trees, gently placing her in front, and pulled out the white box that contained my promise and dedication to only her. I got onto one knee, and began trying to express how much I loved her and how my life had changed for the better since she came into it. How I had searched *years* for someone like her to grow a family with!

Unfortunately, all that came out was blubbering, as my eyes filled up with tears, choking the words I wanted to convey. I would later explain those words I was trying to say in the cab ride home, but the important thing was that when I asked my all-important question, her answer was, "Of course I do!"

That is all I needed to hear, as we made our way quickly back to the waiting cab that would take us to our favorite Italian restaurant called "West 44th" located in Midtown Manhattan. I had reserved our favorite table that included a red velvet plush couch for us to eat our first meal as an engaged couple. We both enjoyed two glasses of red and white wine along with stuffed mushrooms, and two orders of our favorite tri-colored fettucine champignon where chicken was served in a light mushroom cream sauce.

As we walked the short block from the restaurant back to our apartment overlooking Times Square, I quickly reflected on this being one of the best nights of my life because I got to spend it with the girl I had searched and hoped so long for.

CHAPTER 12:
WEDDING DAY APPROACHES

"Do the things that others won't, so your reality is what others dream of."

—Patrick Michaels

In the final months leading up to the special day, I would head home to Buffalo with my beautiful fiancé for a long weekend. Liliana would have a wedding shower and girls' night out with my mother, sister, aunts and female cousins. They would have dinner and drinks at a popular restaurant in Orchard Park called Mangia's, followed by a couple rounds of cocktails upon the establishments new rooftop, overlooking the Buffalo skyline in the distance.

I am so happy she enjoyed her wedding shower with my family and got to share an evening with the strong and wonderful women that make my family so special. I am happy she enjoyed her time in Buffalo, the place that I hold in such high regard.

The following day would be my turn, as I would

have my bachelor party at the Armor Inn Tap Room, sharing the experience with my father, uncles and my closest friends. What a perfect culmination of my single life and preparation for the next step on my journey! This time my journey wouldn't be alone; I would have someone very special to experience the next great moments with, like having children together and creating the family I've been longing for as far back as I can remember.

The night went just as I envisioned, with twenty-eight of my closest friends from all different points of my life in attendance. I had my father and uncles present, whom I have spent my entire life with. They have seen the full transformation. They've seen it all. The peaks and the valleys.

Next, I had my closest friends that I had known as far back as elementary school. I had friends from hockey, friends from high school, and special relatives from Hamilton, Ontario. The night was perfect as we successfully raffled off various top shelf liquors such as Crown Royal and Jack Daniels to Jose Cuervo and Jim Bean. The most popular item of the night and top prize was to the portable grill set that my best man Anthony had purchased, which came with all the accessories from grill utensils to the various popular BBQ sauces that would be perfect for Sunday tailgate before a Buffalo Bills home game.

Overall, the night was special because of the people
that were there, as we reminisced about special times
we had shared. It was great because I was able to spend
more than enough time with each guest, catching up
on current events and any lifestyle changes they were
encountering.

After the bachelor party ended, my best man Anthony and groomsman Tom, along with an old childhood
friend Andy, went on to enjoy a celebratory beer as we
headed towards the fire pits that were outside on the
ground floor. The large patio had four large gas-operated
fire pits that were built to fit fifteen chairs around the
perimeter.

The night even had an unexpected turn of events
when my old childhood friend, Brandon, showed up
unannounced. I assumed he must had seen the Facebook
post made by Andy that described the occasion. I knew
immediately from the moment he came into my view, I
was being tested by the Universe. The Universe wanted
to see if I had truly changed and learned to put away my
past and the friend I had left behind, but still be able to
look him in the eye and shake his hand without feeling or
saying any ill comments towards him.

I accomplished all those things in our brief encounter. I wasn't angry, or hurt, or happy, or sad. Strangely, I felt….nothing. He no longer had a place in my mind or heart, he was in the past and that's where he needed to stay. I spoke to his brother who came up shortly after and he mentioned we were all still brothers and in time things would change.

I have nothing but respect for my friend's brother, but I no longer had feelings to support his claim. We were brothers at one time, closer than family, but things changed. If I let my old friend in again, I was asking for more pain and eventually more hatred towards him and towards myself. If I was going to truly move on, I needed to exclude old friends who no longer added value to my life, nor I to theirs.

As I walked out of the Tap room that night, I felt stronger mentally for successfully passing the test I was given. I held myself to a higher level, as the old me would have started an argument—or worse—and it would have made things more uncomfortable should our paths meet again. As mentioned, I didn't feel anymore hatred or disgust. I just wanted to move on and keep moving forward. I had fully implemented the mindset that I had read so much about and engrained it into my subconscious, and proudly. I was and still am a better person for it.

Chapter 13:
The Culmination

"I don't want to be one of those guys who give their kids all this life advice, but have nothing to back it up. What authority would I have to tell them anything? How can I tell them to go after their dreams if I don't go after mine?"
—Jeff Arch, writer, of the movie *Sleepless in Seattle*

The one thing I wanted to be, above a millionaire, a great athlete, or anything else, is to be a great husband and father. I had waited patiently for the moment to arrive, my wedding day, when the most important chapter of my life would commence. I had found my beautiful bride that I would share my life with, and not too long after the moment had passed, we would start to build our family. As I thought about the major chapter in my life, I thought about the man I wanted to be for Lili and the positive influence I want to have on my future children.

I've had good male role models that have laid the groundwork before me whom I greatly admired, but it would now be my turn to leave my mark on my family name. It would now be my time to take my family to the next level of success, wealth, and above all else, happiness. I want the next generation of my family to take more educated risks, go after their dreams with confidence, and follow the important lessons learned from "The Secret" and the influential books that I have read. I want them to respect the family members that came before them. I want them to be proud of their last name and build upon the reputation for which it currently stands.

I want children, hopefully with at least one son that can continue the family name and take it into the next generation. I want to hold my son in the hospital, on the first day he enters this world, and talk to him about all the things I want to show him. I want my son to enjoy sharing my name, but not feel burdened by it.

I want him to be a proud, respectful, and successful young man. I want him to look up to me and admire our relationship, but make better life decisions that I have made. I want him to achieve great things, and be willing to go after what he wants in this life and know that I am right behind him, pushing him if need be to achieve whatever his "dream scenario" is. I want to communicate well with him, so when I am tough on him, he knows full well that it comes from a good place.

I want him to have a family of his own one day,

where I can spend the golden years of my life taking care of his children and spending holidays with him and his family. I want my son to remember me as a great man, one who wasn't afraid of displaying his imperfect past to the world, but was courageous enough to make a change for the better before it was too late. I want him to see the changes I made, the accomplishments I have and will achieve, and use it as motivation to do the same. I want him to be fearless but calculated. I want him to read this book to his children one day and be proud of the father he had. I want to teach him to be his own person and not follow the crowd, but rather be a class act and be strong in his own skin. Above all else, I want him to be happy.

On this special day, these thoughts flood into my mind. As I waited in the top floor of the White Hall Manor in Bluemont, Virginia, in my private room shared with my father, best man and groomsmen, we reminisced about great moments we had all shared together sitting on the black leather couches and chairs, sipping on the liquor of choice before the biggest event in my life.

My choice on this special day was a single barrel malt of aged whiskey. I calmly put on my tux that was made up of a white tailored suit coat with black trim and black pocket square, black bowtie, finished off with black pants and dress shoes. From the Charles Tyrwhitt British influenced cufflinks, to the freshly polished Johnson and Murphy dress shoes, every fine detail was accounted for.

The moment was at hand, but before I headed up to the altar to greet my guests who have traveled from afar, and moments later my breathtaking bride, I took a few moments to self-reflect and think about the events that had shaped my life. Good or bad, they formed the person that I am today, and honestly, I wouldn't have it any other way.

My mind traveled from the surgery and the alcohol, to the published memoir, to officially owning the Casco Viejo property in Panama, signing the necessary documents just a few days prior, along with committing to the Wollman Rink in Central park, where I will be teaching intermediate to advanced skaters in the upcoming fall back in New York City.

My best man tells me to hurry up, as the mass is about to start, but I take a step back and realize that for the first time in my life, everything has fallen into place. I have a great and supportive family, a strong relationship with my soon to be wife who I would die for, a career I am proud of, and a story that is published and is about to be released to the farthest parts of the world that will help so many.

I take full ownership of my past, current state, and

bright future. I own it all. I think of the ride I've been on and realize that as hard as some moments have been, it all happened for a reason and was necessary for me to meet my current reality. Hearing the wedding music beginning, I knew that it was time to step into my future.

In two short days, Lili and I are off on our honeymoon to the clear blue waters and tropical weather of Bali, where I can spend the next two weeks in the warm sun next to my beautiful wife, where I currently am and will always be…Okay. "Dream Scenario" achieved.